SHIPWRECKS OF ORKNEY, SHETLAND AND THE PENTLAND FIRTH

SHIPWRECKS OF ORKNEY, SHETLAND AND THE PENTLAND FIRTH

by

DAVID M. FERGUSON

© David M. Ferguson 1988

British Library CIP Data

Ferguson, David M.
  Shipwrecks of Orkney, Shetland and
  the Pentland Firth.
  1. Shipwrecks—Scotland—Orkney—
  History   2. Shipwrecks—Scotland—
  Shetland—History
  I. Title
  363.1′23′094113   G525

  ISBN 0 7153 9057 0

Photoset and printed in Great Britain by
Redwood Burn Limited, Trowbridge, Wiltshire
for David & Charles plc
Brunel House, Newton Abbot, Devon

Published in the United States of America
by David & Charles Inc
North Pomfret   Vermont 05053   USA

And make your chronicles as rich with praise
As is the ooze and bottom of the sea
With sunken wreck and sumless treasures
Shakespeare, *Henry V* Act I Scene II

The Swedish motorship *Ustetind* wrecked on Christmas Day 1929 at Coubal, Walls, Shetland. Careful examination of the photograph reveals that the ship's hull had sagged badly. (Shetland Museum)

Contents

List of Illustrations

10

Introduction

While undertaking research for a previous book it became clear that an extraordinary number of shipwrecks had occurred around Orkney and Shetland. To date some 1,500 casualties have been identified, dating from Viking times to the present day. For reasons of space it has therefore only been possible to describe a selection of incidents. The aim has been to present a representative cross-section of shipping casualties down the centuries, related to the changing patterns of traffic and not just to dramatise a few of the more spectacular incidents.

However, no apology is made for writing at greater length about such wrecks as that of the *Suecia*, which is particularly well documented and exhibits most of the features common to shipwrecks of that period – drama, bravery, dishonesty, humanity and avarice.

The text is presented as a general historical narrative, with the more specialised aspects being dealt with in a series of appendices at the end of the book.

A word as to dates – those used are taken from contemporary documents which in the latter part of the seventeenth and early eighteenth centuries could be either New Style or Old Style as they were commonly given in contemporary records without any qualification. For students of the curious it is perhaps worth recording that the Old Style Julian calendar lingers faintly on in Shetland as the inhabitants of Foula still celebrate Yule on 6 January and New Year's Day on 13 January.

Fittingly, though on occasion uncomfortably, a substantial part of this book was written afloat while travelling between Stromness, Aberdeen, Lerwick and Scrabster.

The barquentine *Celtic* of Chester wrecked Bay of Skaill, Sandwick, Orkney 9 August 1907. Her damaged fore topmast, which caused her to become unmanageable, can be clearly seen. (Orkney Library)

Charts of the
Northern Isles
and Pentland Firth
showing wreck
locations

CHART INDEX

SHETLAND

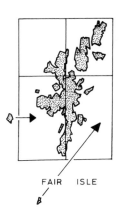

FAIR ISLE

ORKNEY

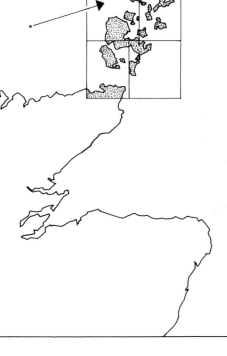

wreck/s = salvaged

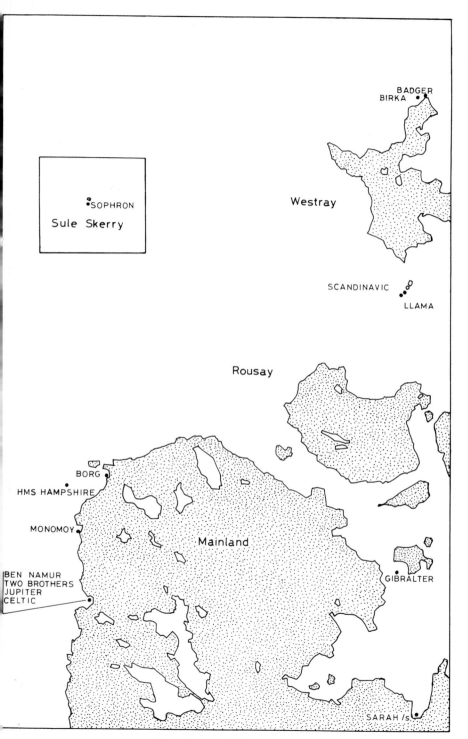

BADGER
BIRKA

Westray

Sule Skerry
SOPHRON

SCANDINAVIC
LLAMA

Rousay

BORG
HMS HAMPSHIRE

MONOMOY

Mainland

GIBRALTER

BEN NAMUR
TWO BROTHERS
JUPITER
CELTIC

SARAH Is.

Northwest Orkney

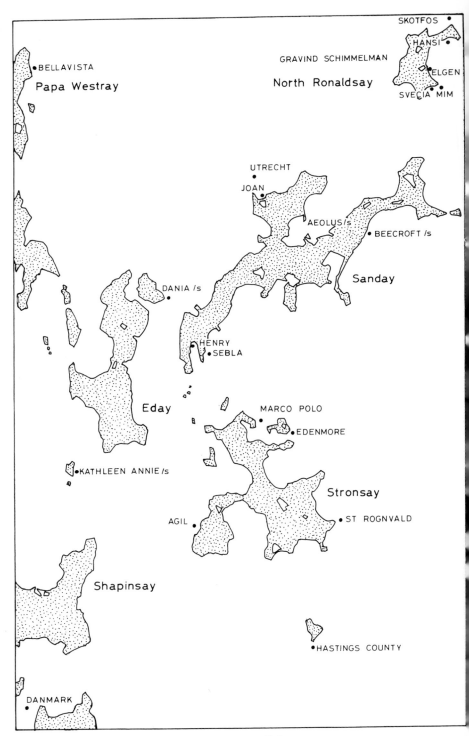

Northeast Orkney

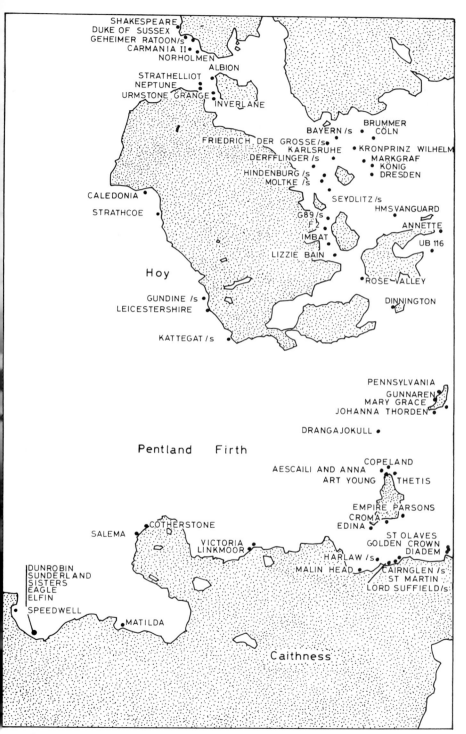

SHAKESPEARE
DUKE OF SUSSEX
GEHEIMER RATOON /s
CARMANIA II
NORHOLMEN
ALBION
STRATHELLIOT
NEPTUNE
URMSTONE GRANGE
INVERLANE

BAYERN /s
BRUMMER
CÖLN
FRIEDRICH DER GROSSE /s
KARLSRUHE
KRONPRINZ WILHELM
DERFFLINGER /s
MARKGRAF
KÖNIG
HINDENBURG /s
DRESDEN
MOLTKE /s

CALEDONIA
SEYDLITZ /s
HMS VANGUARD
STRATHCOE
G89 /s
ANNETTE
F 2
IMBAT
UB 116
LIZZIE BAIN

Hoy
ROSE VALLEY

GUNDINE /s
DINNINGTON
LEICESTERSHIRE

KATTEGAT /s

PENNSYLVANIA
GUNNAREN
MARY GRACE
JOHANNA THORDEN

DRANGAJOKULL

Pentland   Firth

COPELAND
AESCAILI AND ANNA
ART YOUNG
THETIS

EMPIRE PARSONS
CROMA
EDINA

COTHERSTONE
ST OLAVES
SALEMA
GOLDEN CROWN
DIADEM
VICTORIA
LINKMOOR
HARLAW /s
MALIN HEAD
CAIRNGLEN /s
ST MARTIN
LORD SUFFIELD /s

DUNROBIN
SUNDERLAND
SISTERS
EAGLE
ELFIN
SPEEDWELL
MATILDA

Caithness

Southwest Orkney, including Scapa Flow and Pentland Firth

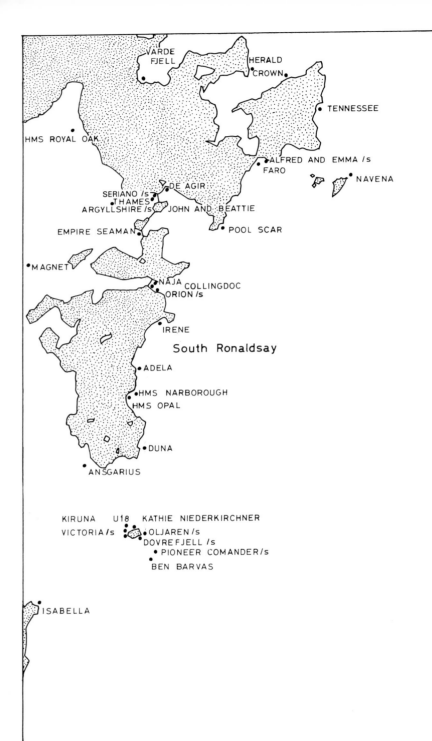

Southeast Orkney, Pentland Skerries and Duncansby Head

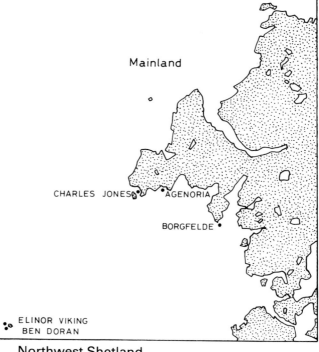

Mainland

CHARLES JONES • • AGENORIA

BORGFELDE •

ELINOR VIKING
BEN DORAN

Northwest Shetland

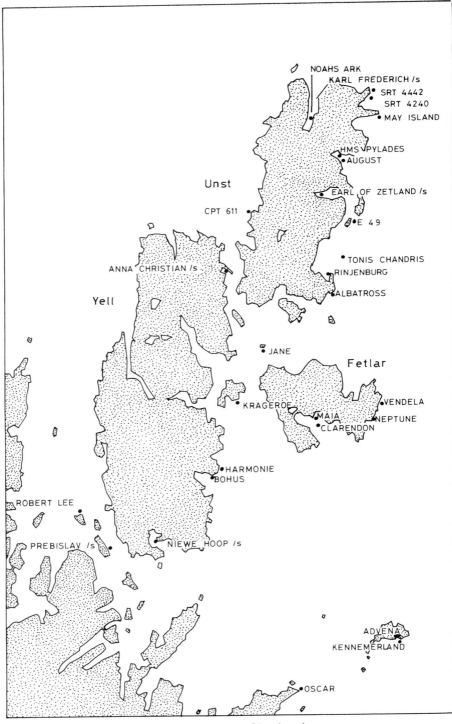

NOAHS ARK
KARL FREDERICH /s
SRT 4442
SRT 4240
MAY ISLAND

HMS PYLADES
AUGUST

Unst

EARL OF ZETLAND /s

CPT 611

E 49

TONIS CHANDRIS
RINJENBURG

ANNA CHRISTIAN /s

ALBATROSS

Yell

JANE

Fetlar

VENDELA

KRAGEROE

MAIA

NEPTUNE

CLARENDON

HARMONIE
BOHUS

ROBERT LEE

PREBISLAV /s

NIEWE HOOP /s

ADVENA
KENNEMERLAND

OSCAR

Northeast Shetland

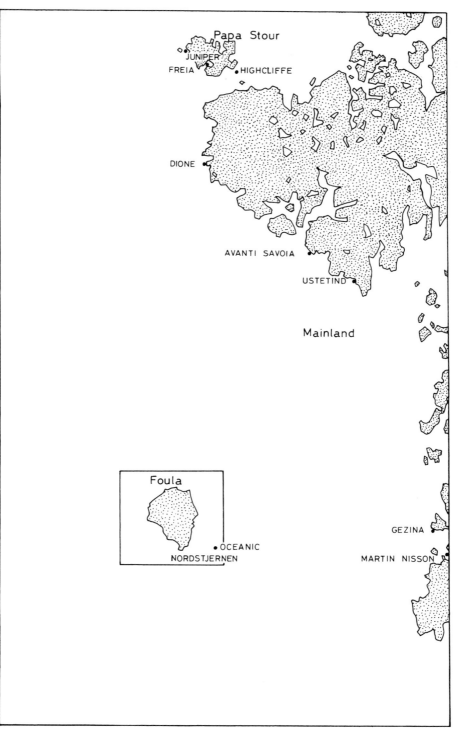

Papa Stour

JUNIPER

FREIA • HIGHCLIFFE

DIONE •

AVANTI SAVOIA •

USTETIND •

Mainland

Foula

• OCEANIC

NORDSTJERNEN

GEZINA •

MARTIN NISSON •

Southwest Shetland including Foula

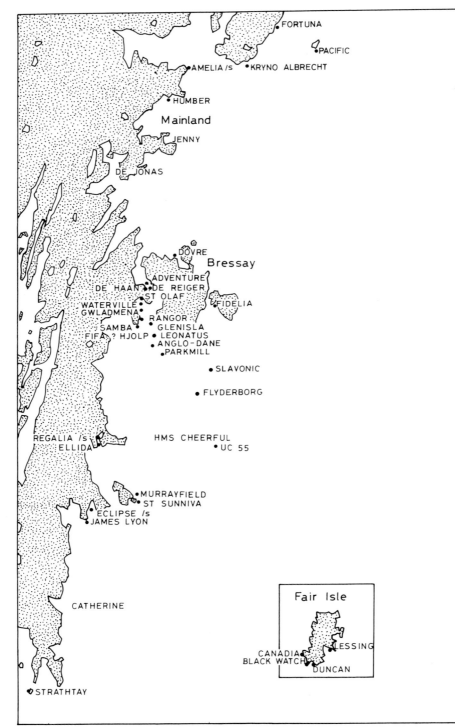

Southeast Shetland including Fair Isle

1

The Pentland Firth and the Northern Isles

In terms of shipwrecks the waters around Northern Scotland, Orkney and Shetland have proved to be some of the most dangerous in the British Isles. Orkney and Shetland lie directly in the path of shipping routes linking Northern Europe, Scandinavia and Russia with the rest of the world. Although now much diminished, a considerable tonnage of shipping still passes through the Pentland Firth, with the oil terminals at Sullom Voe and Flotta handling bulk carriers up to the largest sizes.

With modern navigational aids and a reasonably comprehensive series of coastal lights and signals, modern shipping has little to fear when passing through the area, even in the worst weather conditions. By contrast, in the early days of sail ships' crews literally took their lives in their hands, facing a fearsome combination of tide rips, fogs, reefs and storms in vessels which were all too often ill-found, undermanned and navigating with the aid of charts which were either hopelessly inadequate or grossly inaccurate.

Orkney consists of a group of some seventy islands separated from mainland Scotland by the Pentland Firth. By an accident of geography those islands at the southern end of the group are so arranged as to surround the body of water known as Scapa Flow and form what is virtually an inland sea. This superb anchorage, whose importance was recognised as long ago as the Napoleonic Wars, was a major naval base in the two world wars. Geologically the islands are an extension of Caithness, with underlying sedimentary rocks having eroded to give a subdued topography which was further rounded and softened by several periods of glaciation. Coastlines tend to be relatively low, except on the western side of the archipelago where the action of the Atlantic Ocean has produced a series of spectacular cliffs and stacks, of which the Old Man of Hoy is the best known.

Lying midway between Orkney and Shetland, Fair Isle, also composed of relatively soft sedimentary rocks, is exposed to the full force of the sea on all sides. Except for two landing places the coast consists mainly of precipitous cliffs, stacks and reefs which have taken a severe toll on shipping.

The Shetland Islands form a long narrow archipelago roughly centred between the north coast of Scotland, Norway and the Faroes. The islands have a pronounced north–south grain which reflects the underlying geology and extend some seventy miles from Sumburgh Head in the south to the Out Stacks off the north coast of Unst. Being composed for the most part of hard crystalline rocks of great antiquity, Shetland's topography is a great deal more rugged than that of Orkney. Glaciation and subsequent erosion by the sea, particularly on the Atlantic Ocean side of the archipelago, has produced an extraordinary pattern of islands and skerries with the coasts of the former heavily indented with bays and voes. The western side of Foula has been carved into a series of stupendous cliffs over 1,200ft high and on Papa Stour the sea has tunnelled inland to produce a series of monumental caves, arches and stacks which are unequalled in the British Isles.

The meeting of the Atlantic Ocean and the North Sea produce some extremely dangerous tide rips in the Pentland Firth where the east and west-going streams are constricted, rather like a venturi, between Orkney and the north coast of Caithness. In particular those at the eastern end of the firth have proved lethal to the incompetent or unwary mariner. The best known rip is the Merry Men of Mey race which extends right across the firth from Caithness to Hoy at its full extent during the west-going stream and forms a line of heavy breaking seas even in the calmest weather. With strong to gale force winds blowing against the tidal stream seas of extraordinary violence are produced, putting in peril the best-found ship. It was in such conditions that the First World War British battleship HMS *Albemarle* lost her fore bridge and was completely disabled.

Another exceptionally dangerous race is the Sumburgh Röst extending some three miles to the south of Sumburgh Head. Even in conditions of moderate weather the sea states produced are a hazard to ships of trawler size and below. When the direction of the tide is against that of the wind, particularly when it blows from the west, the confused breaking seas produced present exceptional dangers and are to be avoided at all costs.

In late spring and early summer fogs can blanket the area for days at a time, reducing visibility to virtually nil. With no modern navigational aids, captains of sailing ships were reduced in such circumstances to estimating their positions by dead reckoning which at best was an inspired guess, and at worst fatally wrong. Sanday in Orkney, with its long low coastline almost imperceptible in poor visibility, proved a snare and a graveyard for much early shipping.

Apart from the larger islands, the waters in the area are littered with banks, skerries, shoals and reefs which have taken a desperate toll on shipping. Until a comprehensive hydrographic survey was carried out by the British Admiralty in the nineteenth century, existing charts were woefully inadequate and even today parts of the Pentland Firth remain unsurveyed. However in the sixteenth century Alexander Lindsay's *Rutter of the Scottish Seas*, published about 1540, described the Pentland Firth in considerable detail. For example, 'betwixt Dungisbe and Orkney there is a great daunger causit be nepe tydis whiche is called the Boir' followed by detailed instructions on how to avoid the 'daunger'. Of the early charts of the area, those produced by Captain Greenville Collins and Murdoch Mackenzie are probably the best known. Mackenzie, the son of an Orkney bishop, spent a lifetime charting the seas around north and west Scotland and Ireland. James Boswell, who managed to meet everyone who was anyone, described him in his famous journal as 'a sensible knowing man', surely a major understatement. A local laird, John Bruce of Symbister, undertook on his own initiative the huge task of charting the Shetland Isles at the end of the seventeenth century. His efforts were so successful that those masters of deep-sea navigation the Dutch East India Company had copies of Bruce's charts printed for the use of their own captains.

However, no matter how good the charts might have been they

were of little use in the long black nights of the northern winter. Until
the end of the eighteenth century the coasts of northern Scotland,
Orkney and Shetland were entirely unlit. The toll on North Ronaldsay and Sanday finally proved too horrendous even for the fatalistic
standards of the day and a lighthouse was erected on Dennis Ness,
North Ronaldsay, in 1789 by the embryonic Commissioners for Northern Lighthouses. A list of sixteen vessels wrecked in eighteen years
was compiled for the first Statistical Account of Scotland by the then
incumbent of the combined parish of Cross and Burness (North Ronaldsay and part of Sanday), the Reverend William Clouston, and il-
lustrates the extent of the losses all too clearly. Including a couple of
earlier casualties, he estimated that goods and ships to the value of
some £500,000 sterling had been lost on Sanday and North Ronaldsay during the period, a huge sum for those times.

The light on North Ronaldsay was followed five years later by the
establishment of twin lights on the Pentland Skerries. However, it
was not until 1821 that the first lighthouse in Shetland was erected at
Sumburgh Head. Over the next century a series of lights were built
around the coasts of northern Scotland, Orkney and Shetland and did
much to lessen the toll of shipping casualties.

The North Atlantic is notorious as an area for 'breeding' winter
cyclonic storms and four or five times a year they descend on Orkney
and Shetland. At their most severe they may cause major structural
damage like the Great Gale of 1952 which devastated Orkney. Wind
speeds of over 120mph were recorded before the anemometer blew
away. As a measure of the strength of the wind, a gust removed a
freestone ridge weighing 35lb from the roof of a house under repair in
the Dounby area of Orkney's West Mainland and carried it for over a
mile before it fell in a field. In such conditions definition between sea
and sky is lost and spray is driven across the land like smoke. However, the worst and most dangerous seas are those raised when a gale
has been blowing for several days at a stretch. The waves thus produced hammer on the coasts with quite extraordinary violence and in
areas of strong tidal streams, such as the Pentland Firth or off Sumburgh Head, cause sea states which put the best-found ship in peril.

2

Early Casualties

The earliest recorded shipwrecks in the area are those of the Viking ships *Fifa* and *Hjolp* (*Arrow* and *Help*) which drove ashore together one winter's night in 1148 on the east coast of Shetland, possibly in the region of Gulberwick. They had been gifts from King Ingi of Norway to Rognvald, Earl of Orkney who was returning from Bergen to Orkney with his son Harald. The Orkneyinga Saga chronicles the loss of the two vessels but, apart from the fact that all of those on board apparently survived, only a few tantalising details are given about the wrecks' location. In 1972 an archaeological expedition was mounted to try to locate the wreck site and several sections of coastline south of Lerwick were examined without any trace of the two ships being found. Given the exceptionally active conditions to be found on the shores around Shetland it seems likely that little in the way of artefacts would in fact have survived.

In the 'post-Nordic age', after the transfer of sovereignty to the Scottish crown in 1471, Orkney, Shetland and northern Scotland were infinitely remote from an indifferent government in Edinburgh. Apart from occasional descents by warships and troops in times of national and international upheaval, they were left more or less to their own devices. Coverage of early shipwrecks is in the main superficial and fragmentary but sufficient records survive to allow the researcher to obtain a reasonably clear picture of early shipping casualties.

During the latter part of the sixteenth century the islands of Orkney and Shetland fell under the malign control of one Earl

Patrick Stewart who subverted the legal system, exacted crushing taxes and confiscated property. On 1 October 1592, while on a voyage from his home port of 'Danskene' (Danzig) to Spain with a cargo of 'knappald, wanscoitt, fotheld (?), wode, pypewode and leid', the master of the *Noah's Ark* was forced by 'grite storme of weddir' to run his ship ashore in Burra Firth, Unst. The governor of the island, William Manson, one of Earl Patrick's officials, promptly appropriated the wreck and its cargo and offered the unfortunate master the trivial sum of seventy thalers by way of compensation on a take it or leave it basis. A local landowner, Arthur Sinclair, took pity on the wretched crew who were by now completely destitute and supplied four of them with food at his own expense for fourteen weeks. The owners subsequently brought an action for restitution on grounds of piracy against Earl Patrick before the Lords of Secret (Privy) Council in Edinburgh but this was rejected on a technicality.

In the mid-seventeenth century Spain and the Netherlands were locked in interminable hostilities which were later to be called the Eighty Years War. Notwithstanding this, the Netherlands were the first commercial and maritime power in Europe with the immensely powerful United East India Company (VOC) operating virtually unhindered in the Far East. To prevent the seizure of any of the immensely valuable Retour Vloots or Return Fleets, it was the custom every year to send a detachment of Dutch warships to meet it off Shetland and escort it home. On 15 June 1640 four waiting Dutch warships were surprised in Bressay Sound by a force of ten heavily-armed Spanish frigates. In the ferocious engagement that followed the Dutch ships *Haan* and *Reiger* were sunk at Lerwick, the *Enkhuizen* forced to strike her colours and the *Jonas* escaped to the north. To prevent his ship from being captured by the Spanish, Captain Seger of the *Jonas* ran it aground at Bruntshammarland, Tingwall and had it blown up after his crew had escaped ashore. In 1846, while extensions were being carried out to Lerwick harbour, a quantity of massive oak ship's timbers, partly burnt, was discovered on the seabed. During later dredging operations in 1922, off Alexandra Wharf, more timbers including a 60ft length of oak keel, four cannon and a quantity of cannon balls were recovered. They almost certainly came from the *Haan* and one of the cannon was presented to the Prins

Henrik Museum in Rotterdam. Another, heavily restored and mounted on a new carriage, now lies outside the Shetland Hotel, Holms-
garth, Lerwick.

In Orkney one of the earlier casualties was an unnamed Dutch
vessel described quaintly as a 'bonny and great ship . . . wrackit and
cast away' upon Burness, Sanday in March 1651. With her cargo of
'hyddes, tallow, wax and furis of Russia' she was obviously a valuable
casualty and the Vice Admiral of Orkney appointed various local ship
masters and merchants to make an inventory of the wreck and her
cargo as it was apparently in danger of being pilfered.

Ships of the Dutch East India Company were continuing to use the
more secure 'achter om', or north-about, route due to strained relations with England when the *Kennemerland* sailed in company with
the *Rijnland* for the Far East from the Texel on 14 December 1664.
She had on board over 120,000 guilders in specie and a valuable general cargo when she ran aground on Stoura Stack, Out Skerries in
poor visibility at night on 20 December. According to local tradition
three lookouts who were posted in the rigging were the only survivors
when the foremast fell onto rocks and they were able to scramble
safely ashore. The wreck later broke in two and the stern section was
swept ashore on Bruray.

Due to the severe weather, the 'sad accident was keeped from the
knowledge' of the authorities in Scalloway for twenty-four days.
Later it was claimed that the delay was due to the entire male popu-
lation of Out Skerries having got hopelessly drunk on spirits and
wine recovered from the cargo of the *Kennemerland*. Readers may be-
lieve whichever account they prefer! At that time the islands of
Orkney and Shetland were owned outright, under a grant by the British crown, by William Douglas, Earl of Morton, who sent his Cham-
berlain, William Hunter, to superintend salvage operations. With
'great pains and Trevill . . . thrie little chests with strong iron bandis
and double lockes' and an impressive list of guns, trade goods, ship's
stores and fittings were recovered. Morton made the mistake, apparently a family failing, of retaining some of the items for his own use
and an action was brought by the Crown before the Court of Ex-
chequer in Edinburgh. The case went against the Earl and King
Charles II used this as a pretext to pass an Act of Parliament reclaim-

ing the estates of Orkney and Shetland from the Douglas family. Thereafter the wreck of the *Kennemerland* remained more or less forgotten until 1971 when, in a classic underwater archaeological excavation, initially started by the University of Aston Sub-Aqua Club and lasting for some six years, an astonishing variety of artefacts were mapped and recovered. The artefacts included cannon, brass tobacco boxes, huge numbers of bricks known as 'Overijsselsde Steen', three Bellarmine flagons, coins and, incredibly peppercorns and barley husks.

In the late autumn of 1675 the whaler *St Martin* of Bayonne in France, returning from a successful trip to Greenland, was driven far off course and ran ashore in Caithness. In a Deed of Disposition and Assignation she is stated as 'now lyand in wrack upon the shore of Huna in Canesby' having had on board about 130 barrels of whale oil. In an early example of an employee profit-sharing scheme 'half of the said oyle was to fall and pertaine' to the master and ship's company. In the deed dated 5 December 1674 'Peter Gernoyes, the maister gunner' (apparently the most senior surviving officer) sold the wreck and its cargo so 'as to maintaine me in Cloathes, meat and drink and carry me home to my own native cuntray'.

When the Dutch ship *De Agir* (?) of Hoorn, 'was Brocken upon the rockes under the house of Graemshall', Holm, in the East Mainland of Orkney with a cargo of 'dealls and uther commodities' in February 1678, her master 'Jaan Janssone, was ordered by the Admiral of Orkney and Shetland, Captain Andrew Dick, to appear before him with his crew and produce the ship's papers. After a couple of days' deliberation 'the said ship with her haill loadening (was declared) to be wrecked' and to pertain to the Procurator Fiscal of the Admiralty Court. This meant that the wrecked vessel and cargo could then be disposed of by public roup (auction) with the various court officials taking their cut of the proceeds by way of fees. For example, the best anchor and cable recovered was automatically awarded to the hereditary Admiral of Orkney and Shetland. After all the various deductions had been made the balance from the sale, if any, was paid to the owner. For the Admiral and his court officials the system may be politely described as an exercise in zero risk profit, while for the unfortunate owners it was more often a financial disaster.

The stranding of the *Crown* at Scarvataing, Deerness on the eastern side of Orkney's Mainland in the winter of 1679 was marked by the loss of over two hundred lives in the most deplorable circumstances. She had sailed from Leith on 27 November with over 250 Covenanter prisoners aboard who had been captured at the Battle of Bothwell Bridge. The wretched prisoners had been banished as rebels to 'some one another of our plantations in America' as King James II put it in a letter to the Scottish Privy Council. Originally two vessels were to have been provided but for unexplained reasons only the *Crown* arrived at Leith and it was into her that all the unfortunate Covenanters were crammed. Stormy weather was encountered shortly after sailing and the ship put into Deersound, Orkney, on the morning of 10 December. Her master, Captain Thomas Teddico, ignored local advice to seek a safer anchorage and when the weather worsened on the evening of the same day the *Crown* drove ashore at Scarvataing about a mile to the west of Mull Head 'and the ship was broken all in chatters and small pieces'. The crew managed to get ashore but most of the prisoners, who were battened below deck, were drowned and only about forty or fifty reached the shore alive. Apparently several of them arrived in Kirkwall about a week after the disaster, as a proclamation issued by the Provost and Baillies of the burgh complained that 'some of them have quehered to prejudge and wrong the Inhabitants' who were required to 'arrest any of the said crew'. According to local legend some of the prisoners settled in Orkney and their descendants, such as the Muirs and Deldays, live in the islands to this day. (The proclamation is reproduced on Page 139 and a transcription of the text is given in Appendix D.)

By the end of the seventeenth century English ships were undertaking major deep-sea voyages, particularly to far-flung parts of the then embryonic empire. The *John and Beattie* sailed from her home port of London on 18 September 1690 for a voyage to Barbados. For unexplained reasons, possibly due to adverse weather, her initial course took her north about Britain until the master, David Hugheson, dropped anchor 'in the road of Holmes Sound'. On or about 20 November 1690 the ship was 'by stress and storme of weather driven on shore' on Lamb Holm on the eastern side of Scapa Flow 'wt (sic) great hazard of our lives'. One of the 'Marriners', William Perkins, successfully sued Captain Hugheson for payment of £3 2s. (£3.10) as wages due 'the said ship ... (being) greatly Damnified and prejudged ... and incapable to saill the said voyage'.

The 'barqe' *Joan* of Dundee, was on a somewhat more modest voyage from Bergen to Aberdeen with a cargo of 8½ lasts (about 17 tons) of tar, fourteen hundred deals and nine half hogsheads of brandy in 1706. She cleared Bergen early in November and on 8 November while anchored off Burness in Sanday 'the master and marriners was necessitate to slip his cables for saving ther lives' and drove ashore in a violent southeast gale. She suffered major damage as 'the said ship is wrack and her bottom drung out'. The Admiral Depute, John Traill of Elsness declared the vessel and her cargo to be wrecked and ordered them to be secured on behalf of the owners. However James Traill of West Stove and James Mackie factor (land agent) to the laird of Brough had 'officiously' removed some of the cargo and were fined 500 Scots marks 'per pice'. In mitigation they pleaded that the ship 'was brocken bulk' on behalf of James Sleatter of Hermesgarth before he came to the shore. In February of the following year the *Joan*'s cargo was received on board John Richan's ship 'in Good Condition ... excepting about quarter of an hundred (deals) or thereby' and two casks of brandy.

One of the more unusual ships to be wrecked in Orkney was the Swedish privateer *Sebla* which was 'intirly Stranded and utterly wrack in pices upon Hackness', Sanday, on 30 October 1711. At the time Sweden was engaged in a bitter war with Norway and the *Sebla* had sailed from Gothenburg with a commission from the Swedish Admiralty. Although rather grandiosely described as a 'frigatt', she was in fact only a small vessel (probably a sloop or a galliot) 'of the burden of fifte Tunns or thereby' and must have been extremely crowded with her complement of 'the number of officers and seamen fourtie and seaven men and boys'. Six of her crew were drowned when she went ashore. Her captain, Erik Anderson, petitioned the Admiralty Court in Orkney to dispose of the wreck of the *Sebla* and 'humbly creaved ane pass for him and his men to Goe homeward'. The names of the survivors are listed and amongst them is a Welium Brunn described as a Timmerman or ship's carpenter. Coincidently or otherwise, in 1740 another Swedish ship, the *Suecia*, wrecked in

Orkney, also carried a William Brown as Timmerman.

The Dutch East India Company ship *Rijnenburg* outward bound from Texel for the East Indies was driven ashore at Ham of Muness, Unst, on 15 March 1713 in a violent easterly gale. With the aid of the local inhabitants most of the ship's cargo, including 'ten chests of money and one double chest', was safely brought ashore. Unfortunately, news of these 'immense riches' reached the ear of the Earl of Morton, his estates and perquisite now restored, promptly claimed one fifth of the value of the cargo as salvage fees due even though he had taken no part in the operations. The Admiralty Court in Shetland refused to release the salvaged cargo and specie until the fees were paid although the Dutch had offered to pay all reasonable salvage claims. In July, at the behest of the East India Company, the Dutch envoy in London wrote to the Secretary of State Viscount Bolingbroke, asking that the items should be instantly released. Meanwhile Morton had sailed up to Unst to see the situation for himself and on his return got one of his subordinates, Thomas Gifford of Busta, to submit a huge account totalling £1,260 for his charges on the voyage. This included £500 for his own 'Extraordinary Charge'; hire of 'ane bark and severall boats frauchts' £100, down to Thomas Gifford's own charge of £30 all neatly rounded off to the nearest five pounds. The men actually guarding the cargo were only paid the sum of one shilling (5p) each per day. It was not until January 1714, after protracted negotiations, that the Dutch East India Company finally agreed to pay Morton £800 for the release of the cargo and specie. The company's annoyance becomes even more understandable when they also accused the earl of having removed two chests of silver from another East India ship wrecked in Shetland in 1711 'and applying the same to his own use'.

Scarcely less shifty were the actions of Captain Robert Pearce who described himself as the owner of the *Dolphin* of Dublin 'of old called the *Frollick*, Brigantine' of Dover. On 15 September 1727 Captain Pearce had the misfortune to be wrecked on Stronsay with a cargo of deals and his 'crew' promptly deserted, apparently not even waiting to be paid. Thereafter the good captain was in an unconscionable hurry to have the wreck and her cargo sold 'having urgent Necessary affairs that call him from this place'. In his petition to the Admiralty

Court he asked that the sale should be by public auction and 'your Lordship may allow after ane Inch of Candle is burnt . . . the Sd Ship and Cargo Shall be roupt' (sold). The sale duly took place with the wreck and her cargo being knocked down for £100 and the proceeds going to the dubious captain.

Shipwrecks in times gone by often brought out the worst side of human nature and the loss of the Royal Danish Asiatic Company's ship *Vendela* on Fetlar on 18 December 1737 was an example. She had driven ashore at Heilanabretta on the east side of the island described, aptly as a 'very barbarous place', with the loss of all those on board. The inhabitants of Fetlar quickly discovered that the ship carried large amounts of silver in coin and bullion bars as it had broken up completely. An eyewitness account paints an appalling picture of the havoc at the scene of the wreck; 'the Rocks were full of the legs, Arms and so on and several bodies thrown up by the breach' (of the sea). Salvage operations on the *Vendela*, which was afterwards christened 'the Silver Ship', soon degenerated into an exercise of thieving, cheating and double dealing. One young boy of twelve who had recovered a small brass-bound chest from the shore had it forcibly taken from him by two older boys on Fetlar. An exasperated Procurator Fiscal trying to recover as much of the specie as possible for the unfortunate owners of the *Vendela* discovered one so-called salver had in fact only handed over a third of the coins recovered and kept the rest. In spite of the depredations of the treasure hunters and the primitive equipment used, over three-quarters of the coin and silver bullion aboard the *Vendela* when it sank was in fact recovered.

The seabed where the remains of the *Vendela* lie is exposed and dangerous with large and extremely insecure boulders piled round the site. For this reason no systematic examination of the area has been carried out, but Dr Robert Stenuit a leading underwater archaeologist noted for his work on the Armada wrecks in Ireland has recovered a small number of items which include a few rare and hitherto unsuspected gold coins. It should be pointed out that the *Vendela* is one of fourteen Protected Wrecks under the control of the Shetland Islands Council from whom permission *must* be obtained in advance before any diving can be undertaken. A full list of protected wrecks in the area is given in Appendix E.

While attempting to make the passage between Fair Isle and Orkney, the Swedish East Indiaman *Suecia* drove ashore in a gale on the Reef Dyke lying about a mile and a half to the south of North Ronaldsay on 18 November 1740. A vessel of some 600 tons burden and carrying 28 guns, she had sailed from Bengal three months previously for her home port of Gothenburg with an extremely valuable cargo of bales of silk, cotton goods, dye-wood and saltpetre. The captain had died in India, with another forty-four men succumbing to disease on the voyage home, so the surviving crew were 'obliged to put into Guinea to refresh themselves'.

After the *Suecia* went ashore it was not possible, because of the stormy conditions, for the men on North Ronaldsay to launch boats and rescue the crew which later led the survivors to unjustly describe the islanders as 'barbarous savages'. Soon after she struck, the ship's longboat and pinnace with thirty-one officers and men got away, but they were swept off to the north away from North Ronaldsay. After a hair-raising voyage with make-shift sails improvising from pieces of calico those on board landed safely in Fair Isle next day 'where wee were as well Intertained as the island cou'd afford for 6 pence a day for the sailors'.

The remaining men on the *Suecia* had to make shift to save themselves as best they could. A large raft was constructed from spars and planks and about thirty people, launched themselves on it in the hope of drifting ashore on North Ronaldsay, but it was swept northwards by the tide into a series of terrible overfalls off Dennis Ness and everyone on board was swept off. Some of the others remaining on board made a last despairing attempt to reach the shore by cutting away a section of the deck, but of the twenty-four who trusted themselves to this only thirteen reached the shore of North Ronaldsay safely. One man chose to remain behind; 'the parson ty'd himself to the ship and was lost'. Of the eighty-five people on board the *Suecia* when she struck, only forty-four survived, 'those saved are of the common sort, all Sweeds' as one writer noted with fine flourish of class consciousness. In fact one of those saved was William Brown the ship's carpenter, a native of Portsmouth and it is to him that we are indebted for the eyewitness account of the shipwreck.

A few days later the wreck broke up completely in a violent storm and huge quantities of cargo drove ashore 'the cloth all in pieces among the wrack of the ship and the weeds of the sea'. Due to the stormy weather it was not until the end of November that Admiralty Court officials were able to reach North Ronaldsay and try to prevent pilfering of the cargo which now lay scattered along several miles of coast. At the time Orkney was suffering a particularly severe dearth due to a succession of bad harvests and it was recorded that 'many in the toun (Kirkwall) are next to pereshing for meer want of bread'. The chance of pickings, legal or otherwise, was seized on by the unfortunate islanders like James Graham 'who ran away with a boatfull of goods in the night time'.

Strenuous attempts were made by the authorities to recover the stolen goods and salvage as much of the cargo as possible. It was principally through the efforts of James Fea of Clestrain in Stronsay, appointed principal salver, that something like 200,000yd of material were salvaged, washed and dried in the depths of an Orcadian winter. A further 10,000yd or so of secreted goods were recovered by Warrants of Ranselling and Search or through offers to pay one third of the value of any goods surrendered. Thereafter salvage work was mainly confined to unsuccessful attempts to locate chests of valuables known to have been carried on the ship. In 1976 the wreck site was rediscovered by Mr Rex Cowan and his team of divers who recovered various artefacts which included billets of red dyewood, cannon balls, fragments of fabrics, Portugese coins and a pair of navigational dividers.

The shipping casualties around Orkney and Shetland in the latter part of the eighteenth century were usually on a fairly modest scale in terms of size and value. For example, the snow *Two Brothers* from Boston, Massachusetts was wrecked at the Bay of Skaill, Sandwick, Orkney in October 1746 with a general cargo of dried fish, sugar, tobacco, hides and wood for Amsterdam. Another example was the brigantine *Adventure* of London laden with a cargo of dried fish and driven ashore in a south-easterly storm at Lerwick on 24 September 1762. Her master, James Cooper, 'Protested (against Wind and Weather) In presence of his crew at the main mast'. This, in theory, indemnified the captain and crew against legal claims arising out of loss or damage to the ship or cargo. Just to hedge his legal bets Captain Cooper then went ashore the same day and swore a formal Protest before the Admiral Depute in Lerwick.

Smuggling of contraband goods into Orkney and Shetland during the eighteenth and nineteenth centuries was a major problem for the customs authorities and they deployed a number of schooners and cutters to intercept any vessels engaged in the trade. One such ship was the brig *Princess Caroline*, commanded by Captain John Reid, which ran aground at the south end of Fitful Head in September 1764. By great good fortune the brig drove into a narrow geo or creek from which it was possible for one of the crew to climb to the top of the cliff with a rope. The remainder of the ship's company followed and all managed to get ashore safely. Wreckage from the brig washed out to sea, coming ashore at Walls where the ship's bell was recovered and installed in the parish church.

The East Lands (Russia) were a major supplier of masts and timber for Britain's expanding merchant fleet in the latter part of the eighteenth century. On 10 January 1776 the full-rigged ship *Jenny* of Liverpool bound from Riga in Lithuania with a cargo of masts and logs ran ashore at Eswick, Shetland. All of the crew (variously numbered between twenty-four and twenty-seven) reached shore but, before they could clamber above the tide line to safety, a huge wave swept in and carried away every one of them, except for two ship's boys. Most of the *Jenny*'s cargo was salvaged and shipped to England.

North Ronaldsay was again the scene of a major shipwreck when the Royal Danish West India Company's ship *Gravind Shimmelman* went ashore on 21 December 1781. She had been on a voyage from Copenhagen to St Croix in the Virgin Islands, then a Danish possession, with a general cargo which included provisions, cloth, leather goods and bricks. For unknown reasons her master, Captain Hans Braad, had chosen to anchor off the eastern side of the island and the vessel drove ashore in a gale. The survivors took to the rigging and next day two of them managed to row ashore with a rope. 'A stout yoal' (yawl) carried overland by the islanders to the scene of the wreck was then used to ferry the remaining crew ashore. Some of the survivors appear to have been drunk and disorderly as two of them 'as soon as they landed they began to quarrel beateng and tumbling one another over and over like the wings of a Windmill'. Eventually, in February of the following year, Captain Braad discharged all of the ship's company and sent them back to Denmark.

The unfortunate captain then had to superintend the salvage and disposal of the wreck and her cargo. At the end of operations the island's proprietor, John Traill of Westness, and his tenants submitted huge salvage claims all itemised in vast and minute detail. For example, use of bed and blankets for five months 5s (25p), wet salvage work at 3d (1¼p) per hour and dry ditto 1½d per hour, and postage on express letters at £1 2s 1½d *each*. The lawyers acting for the owners of the *Gravind Shimmelman* replied in suitably outraged terms and offered to pay only one third of the claim. It transpired that Traill had appointed his nephew to superintend salvage operations and the unfortunate young man had drowned along with thirteen companions when their boat sank shortly after leaving Kirkwall. Traill had claimed for all the 'sundries' on board which had been lost, such as one ounce of nutmeg, one and a half pairs of English blankets, six silver table spoons, feather beds, saddles and bridles, carpets etc to the tune of £72 1s 0½d. The case seems to have provided continuing employment for lawyers for many years, though unfortunately the ultimate outcome has not survived among the records.

One of the great hazards of the Pentland Firth for smaller sailing vessels were the immensely strong tidal streams which run at anything up to eight knots. In the case of the sloop *Mary*, which sailed from Longhope in South Walls for Peterhead and Leith on 26 September 1783, the wind suddenly changed direction while the vessel was crossing the Firth and it was swept by the current onto Swona where it grounded and sank. Fortunately the crew managed to get away in the ship's boat and reached Stromness next day.

Although not averse to helping themselves to any item of wreck goods driven ashore, it was unusual for the people of Orkney to go in for the open and wholesale plunder of wrecked ships. However the inhabitants of Sandwick in Orkney's West Mainland, having been cheated, as they thought, a few years previously when they helped salvage a cargo of wood, took the law into their own hands when the sloop *Jupiter* of Wick was stranded at the Bay of Skaill on 22 October

1790. They systematically carried off the vessel's rigging, stores and cargo which included flax, leather, cloth and sugar. Five local men were arrested and taken to Edinburgh for trial before the High Court of Admiralty, but they were all fortunate enough to be acquitted.

During the Revolutionary and Napoleonic wars, which embroiled Britain and France in hostilities for over twenty years, privateers belonging to France and her allies regularly cruised off the northern isles of Scotland ready to seize and carry off any unwary merchant ships. The *Edinburgh Evening Courant* of 31 October 1808 reported for instance that a brig and sloop had been cut out of Widewall Bay, Orkney, by a Danish privateer. It was to prevent such depredations that HMS *Pylades*, a 16 gun brig under the command of Captain Twisden was patrolling off Shetland in late November 1794. On 21 November, in a southeast gale and snow showers, a local pilot was taken aboard off Unst and agreed to take the vessel into the shelter of Uyea Sound. Unfortunately he mistook his bearings and the brig was driven ashore by the storm and totally wrecked in Harold's Wick on 23 November in spite of most of the guns being thrown overboard to lighten the ship. All 124 men of the ship's company reached dry land safely. The subsequent court martial acquitted the captain and officers and found the pilot responsible for the loss of HMS *Pylades*, due to his inexperience and ignorance.

While on a voyage from London to Tonsberg in December 1803 the Norwegian ship *Krageroe* encountered severe weather off Northern Scotland. Her master was obliged to cut away the main and mizzen masts and had to anchor off Whalsay on 23 December. With the weather showing no sign of moderating the passengers and crew abandoned ship and the *Krageroe*, dragging her anchors, was swept on to Hascosay. She broke up and the goods and personal effects driven ashore so completely plundered by the inhabitants of Yell that the passengers and crew were 'rendered so miserable as to be obliged to leave this country'. Matters were sufficiently serious for the Danish Minister in London to make a formal protest to the British Government.

The Dutch frigate *Utrecht* under the command of Captain Albertus Costerus sailed from Helvoetssluis in the company of two other frigates on 15 February 1807, bound for Curaçao with a crew of 230 officers and men and a detachment of 200 artillerymen on board. Having eluded the British blockade and almost made the Fair Isle passage, the frigate was driven completely off course by a violent storm. Early in the morning of 26 February the *Utrecht* was driven ashore in a blizzard on the Holms of Ire off the northwest coast of Sanday. To add to the chaos on board a fire broke out below when the galley stove overturned with the shock of the stranding, though fortunately this was rapidly extinguished. To try to prevent the vessel from broaching-to in the surf two anchors were dropped and the masts cut down. Eventually 366 survivors reached the shore, 54 men having been drowned, died of exposure or killed by surging wreckage. Once ashore the unfortunate Captain Costerus had little choice but to surrender to a local laird.

As the Netherlands were then an ally of France, with which Britain was still at war, the sudden arrival of the Dutchmen caused great consternation in Orkney. Because of the continuing stormy weather it was not until 10 March that the Vice-Admiral Depute, James Watson, with a detachment of fifty men from the Caithness Volunteers reached Sanday to detain the survivors and take charge of the wreck. He found it had been completely stripped by the inhabitants who had carried away everything that they could possibly remove and, a great deal more seriously, had robbed the survivors of their private property and clothes. It has to be said that this is one of only two such cases that I have discovered in reports of over nine hundred shipwrecks in Orkney and Shetland. One captain remarked, having been stranded there in 1774 and having received every consideration from the inhabitants, that if he had to be wrecked again he hoped it would be in Sanday.

The subsequent search to recover goods and equipment from the wrecked frigate uncovered a huge haul of contraband concealed in outhouses, rabbit burrows, stables, dwelling houses and dung heaps. Such impertinent rummagings by the authorities were deeply resented by the islanders, not the least by John Traill, the local laird, whose house at Scar yielded a large haul of stolen goods. Traill, for his part, forbade his tenants from allowing any of the wreck watchers into their homes or any shelter to be built for them on the shore by the wreck. Meanwhile the Dutch survivors were taken to Kirkwall and from thence to Leith where 170 of them elected to enter British service. The remainder were repatriated in April.

The four-masted schooner *Kathleen Annie* of London ashore
on the Green Holm 29 September 1924. (Stromness Museum)

3

Days of Sail

Before the advent of the railways, bulk cargoes were transported round the British Isles by a multitude of small coasting vessels such as sloops, schooners and brigs. The loss rate among them was high. One such vessel, the sloop *Gibralter* of Fraserburgh, Captain William Duncan, ran aground on Seal Skerry between Gairsay and Rendall on 14 February 1823 with a cargo of slates from Easdale in Argyll destined for Leith. Part of the cargo was salvaged, but on 17 February the sloop was washed off the skerry during a southeast gale with her unfortunate master being drowned and the surviving crew having to be rescued from the rigging. According to the salvage accounts which still survive, the labourers and boatmen consumed two gallons of whisky at a cost of £1 2s during subsequent operations. On 17 December the same year the *Margaret* of Aberdeen, probably a sloop or schooner, outward bound from Wick, was totally wrecked on 'Swinna' with the loss of her master, pilot and two seamen. Just over a week later wreckage from the *Margaret* was driven ashore at Birsay in the West mainland of Orkney.

In the space of forty eight hours on 8 and 9 April 1830 no less than three vessels were wrecked on Stroma. The Wick schooner *Edina*, laden with coal and provisions from Leith for Corfu, struck a rock off the west side of the island on the night of 8 April and was totally wrecked. Next day in dense fog the *Aesceili and Anna*, from Arendal for the Isle of Man, stranded off the north end of Stroma, while the *Thetis*, on a voyage from Hull to Quebec, struck on the south end and sank. Fortunately the crews of all three vessels were saved, but only with great difficulty.

Having sailed from Bay Chaleur, Canada, on 5 October 1831 with a cargo of timber for her home port of Saltcoats, the brig *Neptune* encountered such severe weather five days later that the mainmast had to be cut away. The crew abandoned ship on 25 October and were picked up by the barque *Mary* of Colchester. Three months later the derelict brig drove ashore at Braebuster, Hoy on 31 January 1832. A large amount of her cargo was salvaged and sold along with the remains of the hull for £390.

Coinciding with Britain's rise to the peak of military and industrial power in the nineteenth century, her merchant fleet underwent a massive expansion. Vessels of remarkably modest size, such as the 310 ton register *Duke of Sussex*, sailed to the four corners of the earth with cargoes of every conceivable sort. This full-rigged ship, on her maiden voyage, was bound from her home port of Sunderland for the Cape of Good Hope with a cargo of coal and glass. Having sheltered for a few days in Widewall Bay, South Ronaldsay, she was disabled by heavy seas off Cape Wrath on 25 January 1840 and bore up for Stromness to undertake repairs. While trying to enter Hoy Sound late in the same evening she was unable to weather the Point of Breckness and went ashore in a snow storm. The ship broke up almost immediately and her master Captain John Booth, his wife and six of the crew were drowned. It was not until early next day that the seven remaining survivors managed to struggle ashore and obtain shelter in a nearby cottage. The bodies of those lost were later washed ashore and buried in Stromness Kirk Yard. The loss of the *Duke of Sussex* was blamed on the complete absence of lights in Hoy Sound but it was not until 1851 that the lighthouses of Hoy High and Hoy Low were established on Graemsay.

During the mushrooming period of the Industrial Revolution, wood was imported from Scandinavia, Russia and North America in huge quantities to construct ships, mills, and factories and for pit props to support the ever increasing number of coal mines. On the night of 16 December 1842 the barque *Caledonia* of Greenock, laden with a cargo of timber from Canada, drove ashore at Rackwick Bay, Hoy. She had encountered severe gales off Achil Head at the end of November which drove her away to the north past the Hebrides and into the Pentland Firth. With 'their provisions all expended and scare of potatoe to eat' her captain tried to anchor in Thurso Bay but was driven across the Pentland Firth to be stranded on Hoy. Of all the places to go ashore on Hoy's west coast, the bay at Rackwick nestling in a hollow in the huge cliffs was the only one where a shipwrecked crew would have any hope of getting ashore alive. With the help of the crofters who lived there all of the *Caledonia*'s crew managed to reach dry land safely. However, the same crofters were a great deal less than pleased when labourers were brought in from outside to salvage the cargo of timber. The salvage workers were refused any sort of accommodation in Rackwick and had to live in tents on the shore while working on the wreck.

In 1845, with the so-called Railway Mania in Britain at its height, the 136 ton brigantine *James Lyon* laden with a cargo of sleepers for Dublin from Brevick was wrecked on 10 October at Ness of Cumliewick, Sandwick, Shetland. As the terse reports of the time put it 'crew saved with difficulty'. Most of the cargo was later salvaged but the brigantine was a total loss.

Like the *Neptune* before her, the 221 ton snow *Agenoria* of Sunderland had been abandoned in the Atlantic after being disabled in a storm in August 1846. On 4 September the water-logged hulk, with a cargo of wood for St Andrews, drifted ashore at Tang Wick, Hillswick. She was refloated and beached at Sand Wick where the cargo was discharged and reshipped. As the hull of the *Agenoria* was beyond repair it was taken to Hillswick and broken up two years later.

Due to a combination of gales and fog the years 1847 and 1848 were appalling ones for shipwrecks with no less than thirty-eight vessels being lost around Orkney and Shetland. On 14 March 1847 the schooner *Magnet* with a general cargo for Stromness sank after striking the Nevi Skerry in Scapa Flow. During a hurricane on 8 April the brig *Salema* of Glasgow with a cargo of grain was driven from her anchor at Scrabster and went ashore off Dunnet Head. Her mate, the sole survivor from her crew of six, managed to get ashore and then successfully climb a 100 ft cliff at night to save himself. In the same storm the *Wellesley* of Shields with a cargo of coal for New York was driven ashore on Walls at the south end of Hoy with the loss of her crew.

Just over a month later, on 24 May, the immigrant ship *Herald* of Baltimore went ashore at Ness, Tankerness in dense fog with a cargo of coffee and steel and 112 immigrants bound from Amsterdam for the United States. Fortunately, the weather remained calm and all those on board got ashore safely. The unfortunate immigrants were then taken to Leith in June and temporarily lodged in an old sugar warehouse before being returned to Holland. One of the extremely rare instances of survivors being robbed took place on South Ronaldsay when the French brig *Adela* was wrecked at Stews Head on 20 December 1847 with the loss of three of her crew of eleven men. Some of the inhabitants plundered the wreck and robbed the master of his gold watch, a gun and a bag of silver containing 800 francs. Later the culprits were convicted at Kirkwall Sheriff Court and sentenced to sixty days in gaol.

In the winter of 1847–8 Shetland was struck by a series of storms in which a large number of ships were wrecked or severely damaged. On 18 December 1847 the barquentine *Humber* of Hull with a cargo of cotton and cotton goods was wrecked at Howabister, Nesting. On or about the next day an unidentified vessel with a cargo of tar was lost at Gossabrough, Yell. Also driven ashore on 19 December were the barque *Clarendon* of Leith at Wick of Tresta, Fetlar while homeward bound with a cargo of wood; the brig *Amelia* of Kirkcaldy at Stavaness, Nesting with a cargo of hemp and flax bound from Kronstadt to the Clyde and later salvaged along with the cargo, the *Catherine* (nationality unknown) laden with wood which foundered with the loss of all hands off Voe, Dunrossness; and the barque *Oscar* of Hull lost with all hands on Whalsay with a cargo of sleepers from Gothenburg. On 21 December the Norwegian barque *Harmonie* went ashore at Ness of Queyhin, Yell with the loss of one man. The vessel went to pieces in a few minutes and the cargo of stockfish was plundered. Early in the New Year, on 2 January 1848, the Russian barque *Fortuna* with a cargo of wood for Leghorn drove ashore at Isbister, Whalsay, with the loss of eight men from her crew of seventeen. Lastly on 7 January the *Neptune*, a Newcastle-registered barque, was wrecked at Noustaness, Fetlar with the loss of all hands, part of her hull and name board being washed ashore later.

Fortunately, later shipping losses around Orkney and Shetland were never on the same scale as those of 1847–8, the improvement being in some measure due to the slowly expanding network of coastal lights. One of the more bizarre casualties was the Norwegian brig *Annette* which foundered in a storm off Orkney in March 1850 with a cargo of American sugar for Copenhagen. Later in the month she was discovered waterlogged and derelict off North Ronaldsay, the cargo having dissolved, allowing the sunken ship to float back to the surface! The *Annette* was towed to Kirkwall and later advertised for sale in the local press.

The Pentland Firth's tides continued to take their toll when the Newcastle-registered barque *Diadem* ran ashore at Ness of Duncansby on 4 April 1852 in a moderate wind and good visibility. She had been on a voyage from Shields to Montreal with a general cargo which included glass, chemicals and paint when she took a sheer on the flood tide off Duncansby Head, failed to answer her helm and went ashore. The barque filled within ten minutes but the crew of thirteen all reached shore.

In January 1854 the 333 ton register Liverpool barque *Charles Jones* loaded a general cargo including a consignment of railway iron at Leith for Valparaiso. She sailed towards the end of the month with the master's wife and children on board. On 31 January the vessel was driven ashore at the Hole of Stuvva, Eshaness and broke up completely with the loss of all those on board. It was not until a bundle of papers was recovered from the shore that the identity of the wreck was established, so complete was the destruction. One of the larger sailing vessels to be wrecked in Orkney was the 1,300 ton full-rigged ship *Annette* of Bordeaux (sometimes referred to as the *Anita*) which went ashore on Roan Head, Flotta on 14 December 1858. Her rudder had been carried away in a gale while on a voyage to Valparaiso with a cargo of Swedish timber which was salvaged and sold by public auction the following June. The sale attracted widespread interest with hundreds of potential buyers descending on the island, which did not even have an inn. As the *John O'Groat Journal* put it: 'He was a fortunate man who could reckon upon being one of three in a bed, while others betook themselves to couches or chairs and the softest plank on the floor.'

On 19 December 1862 Northern Scotland was struck by a storm

which caused immense damage both ashore and at sea. At Thurso six vessels were driven ashore, though apparently without loss of life. They were the *Eagle*, schooner of Wick, with a cargo of tiles for Forss; the *Elfin*, brigantine of Girvan coal-laden for Dublin; the *Matilda* of Thurso (type unknown) laden with oilcake and coal; the *Sisters*, a Wick schooner; the Norwegian schooner *Sunderland* timber-laden for Whitehaven and the *Dunrobin* (type and cargo unknown). The last named was driven so far ashore that she ended up in a field, but was described as being repairable!

Like most subsistence communities by the sea, the inhabitants of Shetland had fairly easy-going notions about the ownership of wrecks and wreck goods cast up on their shore. Thus when the galliot *Gezina* of Emden, later to be christened the 'Shuggar Ship', was seen drifting down, damaged and abandoned, onto the southwest side of St Ninian's Isle, Dunrossness on 9 March 1863 the inhabitants of Bigton and Scousburgh put off in their boats to try and board the casualty. She had in fact grounded earlier that day in suspicious circumstances on the west side of Fitful Head while on a voyage from Hamburg to Memel with a cargo of sugar, champagne and iron pots. Almost immediately after being abandoned by her crew with a broken bowsprit and jib-boom the vessel had floated off and was swept north by the ebb tide towards St Ninian's Isle with the master and crew in hot pursuit in the ship's boat. In the meantime some local men had managed to board the *Gezina* and bring up the vessel just short of the rocks. However, immediately after the captain got back aboard his ship the kedge cable parted, having apparently been deliberately cut by him, and the galliot drifted ashore.

Having decided that there was no further point in trying to save the ship, the local men proceeded to plunder the *Gezina* and made off with her fittings, cargo and stores. Acting on a complaint made by the captain, a major search was mounted of the district to try and recover the stolen items and arrest those responsible. A considerable quantity of sugar, ropes, fittings and so on was found and several men including, to the embarrassment of the authorities, an assistant to the local Receiver of Wrecks were eventually taken into custody at Lerwick. The investigation was greatly hampered by the complete unwillingness of the local people to implicate one another and eventually the

legal proceedings fizzled out with all of those in custody being released without having to stand trial.

In November 1864 Shetland was again hit by an appalling
southerly storm with about twelve vessels being driven ashore, of
which only one was subsequently refloated. The total does not
include ships which foundered at sea with only some unidentifiable
wreckage being driven ashore later, as accounts of the storm speak of
huge amounts of floating wreckage being sighted in the North Sea for
weeks afterwards. Contemporary reports vary somewhat as to dates
and the number and identities of the vessels wrecked, but, as far as
can be established, the first casualty was the large Russian three-
masted schooner *Libra* which went to pieces on the Out Skerries on
24 November. Her crew was saved and wreckage from the schooner
laden with a cargo of coal for Stockholm was later washed ashore on
Yell and Unst. Next day, 25 November, the Norwegian barque
Freia, in ballast from Aberdeen to Fredrickstad, was driven ashore
and totally wrecked at Hamna Voe, Papa Stour, though fortunately
without casualties.

On the same day another two ships went ashore at Aith Voe, Cunningsburgh, while trying to shelter from the storm. The Norwegian
schooner *Ellida*, with the crew lashed to their stations to prevent
them being washed overboard, had almost reached the safety of the
voe when she was struck by a huge wave and driven onto a reef. The
masts immediately went by the board in the huge seas and the crew of
six men and a boy were drowned. Not long afterwards the 156 ton
snow *Regalia* of Amble managed to get safely through the entrance
and her master, Captain Hall, ran her ashore on a sandy bottom at the
head of the voe. The *Regalia*, on a voyage from Ystad to London with
a cargo of grain, was refloated on 6 December and was the only vessel
to be salvaged.

Another two ships went ashore on 26 November, an unnamed
Danish schooner being driven into Sand Wick, Dunrossness, and a
large vessel of 600–800 tons, believed to be Norwegian, went to
pieces on Trebister Ness, Gulber Wick. In the case of the schooner
the crew managed to drop both anchors and cut down the masts
before passing a line ashore. A warp was then hauled aboard along
which the crew were able to reach the shore safely. At Gulber Wick

there was no trace of any of the crew and it seems probable that the vessel had been abandoned at sea. The wreck soon broke up and huge quantities of deals and battens from the cargo filled the bay to be flung ashore in huge heaps mixed with wreckage from the ship.

On 27 November the Norwegian schooner *August*, laden with a cargo of coal for her home port of Christiania, having been disabled in the storm and then embayed, was run ashore by her captain at Harold's Wick, Unst, with the crew of six being saved. The Prussian schooner *Fidelia* also went ashore the same day on the south side of Noss. As she was being driven towards the shore the masts were cut down and one of them fell on the rocks enabling the crew to scramble ashore along it. The *Orcadian* of 13 December 1864 reported that the wreckage of two vessels had been discovered on Burra Isle along with items such as boxes of women's and children's clothing, a clock, a hen coop, beds and some letters being picked up on the coasts of Yell and Unst. Together with miscellaneous wreckage picked up elsewhere it seems likely that at least twelve ships were wrecked in Shetland during that particular storm.

The west coast of Orkney's mainland was the scene of a major shipwreck when the full-rigged ship *Albion* of Bristol stranded on the Point of Oxan, Graemsay, on New Year's Day 1866. She had encountered severe weather shortly after sailing from Liverpool on 19 December bound for New York with forty-three passengers and a general cargo and had been driven northwards far off course. By the time the *Albion* was off Orkney most of the sails were ripped to shreds and the crew were exhausted from having had to continually man the pumps and work the ship. For unexplained reasons her master, Captain Williams, dropped anchor in Hoy Sound off the western end of Graemsay in a westerly gale and blinding snowshowers. Two local pilots put off to try to persuade the captain to cut his cables and run for shelter, but before anything could be done the ship dragged her anchor and ran shore.

As no lifeboat was then stationed in Orkney, a flotilla of small boats immediately put off to rescue the passengers and crew as the *Albion* was rapidly breaking up. Tragically, during the rescue one boat overturned and ten of its occupants, including a young Graemsay man, Joseph Mowat, were drowned. By evening the ship had broken up completely and the beach was strewn with pieces of wreckage and the remains of the cargo of tinplate, bricks, stoneware, bales of cloth and bar iron. A little was subsequently salvaged. At least one house in Stromness still sports a selection of heavy earthenware dishes recovered from the wreck and to this day the beach at the Point of Oxan is still strewn with fragments of stoneware. As a direct result of the disaster the Royal National Lifeboat Institution established a lifeboat station at Stromness in 1867.

Although small, Fair Isle lay directly in the path of trans-Atlantic shipping routes to and from Northern Europe until the advent of steam power changed the routes commonly taken. For this reason this little island took a horrendous toll on sailing ships, claiming over forty recorded major casualties. The largest sailing vessel ever to be wrecked there was the 1,800 ton immigrant ship *Lessing* of Bremen which ran aground in thick fog at Clavers Geo on 23 May 1868. Incredibly there were no casualties. The crew and 465 German immigrants on board were all taken off in boats manned by Fair Isle men. In order to rescue the people the boats had to negotiate a natural arch in the cliff which was so low that those on board were in danger of being crushed against the roof. All of the survivors were later taken to Lerwick and quartered in Fort Charlotte before being returned to Bremen in a specially-chartered steamer. The Senate of Bremen later voted for a reward of £100 to be distributed amongst the rescuers on Fair Isle.

Apart from the more usual cargoes of wood, coal, salt and so on, several of the ships wrecked in the area were carrying consignments of ice from Norway to Britain, an important commodity for preserving fresh food in the days before the invention of refrigeration systems. On the morning of 8 February 1870, having experienced a month of appalling weather in the North Sea, the Norwegian brig *Henry* with a cargo of ice for London was driven ashore at Hacks Ness, Sanday. In the heavy seas that were running it was not possible for a boat to put off and, as she lay on rocks some distance from the shore, there was no way a line could be put aboard. The unfortunate crew had to save themselves as best they could and of the ten men on board only three reached the shore alive, several of those lost having been crushed by the ice from the cargo.

Fair Isle again claimed a major casualty when the full-rigged ship *Black Watch*, 1,319 ton register of Windsor, Nova Scotia, was wrecked at Shalstane on 19 September 1877. She had been carried ashore in light airs by the tide and was on passage from Bremerhaven to New York in ballast with twenty-three passengers and crew on board. All on board reached shore safely but the ship, only four months old and valued at £11,000, became a total loss.

Apart from the *Gezina* only one other ship is known to have been deliberately run ashore in Orkney and Shetland. After being sailed in an apparently aimless manner off Kirkwall, on 5 October 1877 the barquentine *Agil* of Prince Edward Island was deliberately put ashore on the Little Green Holm, south of Eday, by her master Captain Henry Bennet. Two days later the barquentine floated off at high water and was driven before the wind and tides to ground on rocks at Rothiesholm Head, Stronsay. It was clear from the start that the *Agil's* stranding was not accidental and the *Orkney Herald* reporting the sale of the wreck, drily noted some of the eccentric proceedings – 'one gentleman pacing the strand in undisguised wrath, shouting for a five shooter revolver ready loaded to "shoot the white caps" with'.

At the subsequent Board of Trade inquiry the captain's certificate was cancelled after it had been revealed that most of the crews' testimony was false, the log had been tampered with and, most damning of all, several large holes had been bored in the bottom of the ship. But just what was behind such an amazing string of irregularities was not recorded.

In summer, with long hours of daylight and relatively settled weather conditions, seafarers still had one major hazard to contend with. Fog could reduce visibility to virtually nil for days at a time. The unfortunate Captain McLean of the Liverpool barque *Pool Scar* was ten miles north of his estimated position when he grounded in dense fog at Rose Ness, Holm early in the morning of 26 June 1880. The 1,032 ton net barque had been on a voyage from Bremen to Quebec with 120 tons of general cargo which included steel wire and a consignment of toys. Her crew of eighteen and two stowaways reached shore but the *Pool Scar* was a total loss. The wreck and cargo, or what was left of it, was sold for £207, the inhabitants of Holm, reported a scandalised *Scotsman*, having stripped the wreck of anything moveable before the sale.

By the latter part of the nineteenth century Lerwick had become a major herring fishing port with thousands of barrels being shipped to the Continent every year. On the evening of 21 November 1881 the 139 ton Wick schooner *St Olaf* was on passage to Lerwick to load a cargo of herring for the Baltic when her master mistook the lights of the town for ships lying off the port. Although he realised his error and dropped anchor, the schooner dragged and went ashore at The Slates, Brei Wick, on the south side of Lerwick. The crew were able to save themselves in the ship's boat but the *St Olaf* was completely wrecked.

In the late nineteenth and early twentieth centuries small fleets of schooners, cutters and sloops traded around Orkney, Shetland and the coasts of the western highlands of Scotland acting as floating shops. The *Lizzie Bain*, a sloop belonging to the Kirkwall merchant firm of Messrs Garden, was one of these 'shop boats' and used to make weekly trips around the South Isles of Orkney exchanging groceries, china, boots and clothing for shellfish, eggs, wool, butter and so on. On the night of 6 November 1888, while anchored without riding lights in the fairway between Fara and Rinnigill in North Walls, she was run down by the local steamer *Queen* with loss of the crew of three. Today, little remains of the wreck except for a scattering of crockery on the seabed.

By the beginning of the twentieth century sailing ships were becoming a thing of the past, but a number of smaller vessels were still to be seen in the waters around Orkney and Shetland, typically carrying bulk cargoes in 100–200 ton lots. The steel three-masted Swedish schooner *Dione*, a new vessel built only in 1904 sailed from Elsinore with a cargo of deals and battens for Tarragona at the end of December 1905 and encountered severe weather while going north-about the Shetland Islands. Her captain decided to seek shelter and tried to anchor in the Voe of Dale, but was driven ashore early in the morning of 15 January 1906. The captain and two men were drowned trying to reach the shore and the mate was killed by floating wreckage. As there was no life-saving apparatus in the area at the time it was only with great difficulty that a line was passed to the three survivors still on the wrecked schooner and although all three were finally brought ashore, one subsequently died of his injuries.

The iron barquentine *Celtic* of Chester bound with a cargo of cement from London to Oban was disabled in a gale off Orkney on 9 August when her fore topmast snapped rendering her unmanageable. Before the wreckage could be cleared she had drifted before the wind and gone ashore in heavy seas at the Bay of Skaill on the west coast of Orkney. Her master, Captain Hall, was almost immediately washed overboard though fortunately he, like the rest of the crew, was wearing a cork life jacket which kept him afloat. The remainder of the crew then jumped overboard and were swept ashore to be rescued, somewhat cut and battered, by local people who had gathered to render assistance. In the exposed position where she lay the *Celtic* rapidly filled with water and in less than a week was declared a total loss. Somewhat optimistically the wreck and her cargo were advertised for sale in February of the following year.

The largest sailing vessel ever to be wrecked in Orkney was the full-rigged ship *Edenmore* of Greenock, 1,726 ton gross, which went ashore on Papa Stronsay in October 1909. Having loaded a general cargo which included pianos, furniture, chemicals and machinery at Hamburg she set sail for Sydney on 3 October. Shortly before midnight on 7 October the *Edenmore* ran hard aground on the Rhone off the south-east point of Papa Stronsay. Distress flares were sent up but the crew were only rescued with great difficulty as the Stronsay Lifeboat was under repair in Kirkwall and the local fishing boats were far too small to carry all the survivors in the heavy swell. One of the larger boats, manned by lifeboat men, succeeded in getting alongside the *Edenmore* and persuaded her crew to launch the ship's boat which was taken in tow. With the twenty-five survivors divided between them they managed, after some very hard rowing, to reach the safety of Whitehall harbour in Stronsay. Over the next three weeks a considerable amount of cargo including twenty-three pianos (shipped sealed in tin plate containers), 23,000 slates and a quantity of chinaware was recovered. The *Edenmore* finally broke up completely on 5 December after a north easterly gale. A considerable amount of chinaware was later salvaged from the wreck and at one time most of the houses in Stronsay had their souvenir of the *Edenmore*.

The 472 ton brigantine *Advena*, with a cargo of coke for her home port of Kalmar, was struck by a huge wave at the south entrance to the Out Skerries while trying to shelter from a hurricane on 18 January 1912. She was flung onto rocks on the western side of the entrance, her masts immediately went by the board and within ten minutes she had sunk. Although a boat manned by Skerries men immediately put off in the appalling weather only two survivors from the crew of seven were picked up. One of the rescuers said afterwards that the cries of the men on the wreck were so terrible that they could be heard clearly above the storm and the roar of the breaking waves. In 1971, during operations to relocate the wreck of the Dutch East Indiaman *Kennemerland*, an American-made spirit-filled compass was recovered from the bottom of Skerries Harbour which probably came from the *Advena*.

Hard aground and wedged between two rocks, the Wick schooner *St Olaf* wrecked at Slates, Lerwick 21 November 1881. (Shetland Museum)

The full-rigged ship *Edenmore* hard aground on the Rhone, Papa Stronsay 7 October, 1909. (Orkney Library)

The stern section of the steamer *Dinnington* which went ashore on Switha, 16 February 1906. (Stromness Museum)

4

Days of Steam

The first steamship to be wrecked in the islands was the 1,292 ton Liverpool-registered *Pacific* which went ashore on East Linga off Whalsay on 7 February 1871. Shortly after sailing from Norway on 29 January, bound for Hull, she lost her propeller in heavy weather and drifted helplessly before the wind across the North Sea. In hurricane force winds the steamer was driven onto a reef about half a mile off East Linga and broke in two. Of the crew of twenty-eight only the captain and two seamen survived when they were washed ashore on the foremast. As the island is uninhabited the survivors had to take refuge in an empty fisherman's hut and subsist on grass and shellfish for four days before they could be rescued by a boat from Whalsay.

With the coming of steam power many of the dangers associated with sailing vessels were removed, but fog remained a major hazard until the introduction of commercial radar in the 1950s. Until then ships were reduced to groping their way through the fog at reduced speed with lookouts posted in the bows. The steamer *Duncan* of Dundee was far off course when she ran ashore on Fair Isle on 19 July 1877 in thick fog while outward bound to Archangel in ballast. At that time there were neither lighthouses nor fog signals on the island. Only a week before the stranding a Captain Prouse had visited Fair Isle on behalf of the Board of Trade to discuss the proposed installation of rocket apparatus. Fortunately the weather remained calm and all of the crew, and a clergyman travelling as a passenger, were able to get ashore. Practically nothing was salvaged from the *Duncan*, but six days after she had grounded her bell, attached to part of a wooden beam, was washed ashore on the island of Oxna off Scallo-way, having drifted forty miles. Fog was also responsible for the loss of the steamer *Cotherstone* of London, which ran aground on Dunnet Head early on the morning of 29 August 1887. Given the fickle and complex currents whose reputation is notorious among seamen, her master Captain George Wild, was unwise to say the least in trying to pass through the Pentland Firth at night in zero visibility. Fortunately all his crew reached shore, but the steamer, in ballast from Dublin to Sunderland, was a total loss.

Early steamships had a tendency to be underpowered and it would appear that the *Borgfelde* of Hamburg grounded on Brucie's Baa, Hillswick, in 1888 because her engines were unable to maintain steerage way in the strong currents off Ness of Hillswick. Shortly after sailing from Hillswick with a local pilot on 7 July, carrying a cargo of 3,325 barrels of herring and twenty passengers for Stettin, the vessel became unmanageable and ran ashore, both ship and cargo becoming a total loss. A few days later on 25 July the 439 ton registered *Copeland* of Leith, homeward bound from a voyage to Reykjavik with a cargo of dried fish, wool and 480 ponies, ran aground at full speed in dense fog on Langaton Point, Stroma. Earlier, Captain Thompson had stopped in the Pentland Firth and taken on board a fisherman to despatch a telegram to the owners in Leith. The fisherman's offer to pilot the *Copeland* through the Firth was declined and, after returning him to his boat, the steamer proceeded on her way at full speed. She ran aground shortly afterwards and was badly holed forward, remaining fast in spite of the engines being put full astern. Her eleven passengers, one of whom was the well-known writer Rider Haggard, were sent ashore in the ship's lifeboat. The ponies were put over the side to swim ashore as best they could, but over 120 drowned. Those that reached shore on Stroma were able to find adequate grazing on the island and were little the worse for their dip. Within a week the *Copeland* had broken in two with the stern section sinking in fourteen fathoms of water and the bow lying on a reef. At the subsequent Board of Trade inquiry Captain Thompson declared that, at the time of the stranding, he had been continuously on watch for over twenty-four hours and had not taken his clothes off for five days.

The Protocol Book of Peter Keith, a Thurso solicitor, preserved in Inverness Library Archives contains, apart from its more prosaic correspondence, 'A Protest against Wind and Weather'. This declaration duly signed and witnessed was made by Captain Duncan Leitch master of the 80 ton Glasgow steamer *Speedwell* when his vessel drove ashore at Scrabster on 6 January 1892. She had been sheltering in Scrabster harbour from a northeasterly storm while on a voyage from Stornoway when the mooring ropes parted and the vessel was blown ashore and completely wrecked. Captain Leitch's 'Protest' was, under Scottish law, to help protect him from any legal claims arising from the loss of the ship.

Nothing is known of the circumstances of the loss of the little wooden steamer *Ino* of Stavanger which disappeared with all hands some time in early January 1893. She had been on a voyage from Ardrossan to Norway with a cargo of coal and is presumed to have grounded on either Sacquoy Head, Rousay or the Skea Skerries south of Westray. Huge quantities of wreckage were washed ashore at points as far apart as Deerness in Orkney's East Mainland and Papa Westray in the North Isles and although two bodies were found it was not until a lifeboat carrying the ship's name was recovered that the wreck could be positively identified. The vessel must have gone to pieces immediately on striking as the precise location still remains unknown.

Another wooden-hulled steamer, the *Ansgarius* of Stavanger with a cargo of coal for Christiania, was wrecked when she ran aground on the Lother Rock off South Ronaldsay at full speed early in the morning of 30 August 1895. Although it was blowing a full gale and she sank almost immediately, her crew managed to escape in two lifeboats. One, containing six men, came ashore safely at Burwick in the southern point of South Ronaldsay, but the other, with the master and six men, was swept out past Halcrow Head before being capsized by heavy seas. The crew managed to get back aboard the boat, but the oars were lost and it was only with great difficulty that they managed to prevent the boat from being smashed on rocks. Eventually, one man swam ashore to find help and the survivors were towed into Windwick Bay by the local boatmen. In the meantime the mate and one of the seamen had become insane and died in the boat – the body of the latter was thrown overboard, that of the mate was brought ashore and buried in the South Parish churchyard, South Ronaldsay.

One of the most famous shipwrecks in Orkney was that of the 1,792 ton register Bristol steamer *Monomoy* which ran aground in Marwick Bay early in the morning of 6 January 1896. The ship was on a voyage from New York to Leith with a general cargo and encountered patchy fog at the western end of the Pentland Firth. Her master, Captain Duck, wisely decided to stand out to sea again and wait for daybreak before attempting to pass through the Firth, but unfortunately he neglected to first check the ship's position and shortly after changing course the ship ran aground at ten knots. There was little ground swell so the chief officer was sent ashore in a lifeboat to obtain assistance from Stromness. Later the same morning the remainder of the crew were taken off by the lighthouse tender *Pole Star*. As the steamer was hard aground with no chance of being refloated, every effort was made to salvage the cargo. However, salvage had to be suspended after a few days when a severe gale broke the *Monomoy*'s back. Such huge quantities of cargo came ashore that parts of the beach were six feet deep in places with a mixture of wheat, bags of flour, gig spokes, pick handles, rolling pins and casks of lard. The wheat was sold on the spot as 'hen's meat' at a penny a bag, though no one enquired of the hens if they liked their food extra salty! Sacks of flour were also sold from the beach at 1s 6d to 6s each, it having been discovered that, after initial wetting, the outer portion of the contents formed a waterproof crust which kept the interior reasonably dry. The rolling pins were in great demand and there were very few local kitchens which did not acquire this souvenir of the *Monomoy*. Surprisingly, the wreck was sold by public auction for £210, although by then the ship had almost completely broken up. Having lain submerged for almost ninety years, the ship's boiler was washed up on the beach at Marwick Bay in January 1985 after a spell of severe westerly gales!

The last wooden-hulled steamer to be wrecked in Orkney was the 360 ton *Elgen* of Stavanger which ran aground in thick fog on the Reef Dyke, North Ronaldsay on 1 June 1897 with a cargo of ice for Glasgow. This slightly curious vessel was also rigged to carry sails on her two masts, not an unusual feature on early steamships whose engines were less than reliable. After reaching shore with her crew, the master returned to the wreck with some local boatmen and found it had floated off and was drifting with the tide almost completely submerged. The *Elgen* was taken in tow by two boats and beached in Linklet Bay after some very hard rowing. Later in the month the wreck was sold for £158 and the boatmen brought a successful action in Kirkwall Sheriff Court and were awarded £2 each as salvage money.

By the end of the nineteenth century a huge tonnage of shipping, a substantial part of it British, was passing through the Pentland Firth annually as trade between Northern Europe and the rest of the world increased dramatically, but by modern standards navigational aids were still primitive and the Firth continued to be extremely hazardous, especially in times of poor visibility. Thus it was in thick fog that the Arrow Line steamer *Croma* ran aground on the south east side of Swona on 13 August 1899, outward bound from Dundee with a general cargo for New York. Customs officers were quickly on the scene as part of the cargo included a consignment of beer and spirits and this was duly recovered. As the *Croma* had gone aground at high tide there was no chance of refloating the ship. By the middle of September when she broke up and sank in deep water, over 300 tons of cargo had been recovered. This was sold by auction on Stroma with 4,816 cases of marmalade fetching 6s 9d–7s 6d each and canvas £1 per bolt.

Britain's fishing industry underwent a massive expansion in the last quarter of the nineteenth century with steam trawlers and liners exploiting the rich fishing grounds off Orkney, Shetland, the Faroes and Iceland. Most were modest in size like the little *Albatross* of Hull, 156 tons gross, which foundered with the loss of all hands in a storm off Unst in December 1899. Two bodies and part of a ship's boat were recovered at Noustigarth, Muness on 29 December, with more wreckage coming ashore at Sumburgh early the following year. In February 1900 Northern Scotland was struck by an appalling storm. At one time five trawlers being unaccounted for and huge quantities of wreckage and fishing gear were being washed ashore along the coasts of Orkney and Shetland. One of those lost was the *Strathtay* of Aberdeen which ran ashore on Horse Island off Scatness on 16 February 1900. Flares had apparently been seen off the island on the night of the tragedy, but no attempt was made to raise the alarm and, apart from some unidentified wreckage, there was no trace of ship next day. In fact it was not until 1977, over three quarters of a century later, that she was positively identified when some wreckage, carrying a numbered builder's name plate, was washed ashore at Sumburgh and Messrs Hall Russell of Aberdeen were able to confirm that it belonged to the trawler *Strathtay* which they had built in 1892.

At about 6am on 24 April 1900, while on her scheduled run from Lerwick to Kirkwall, the mail steamer *St Rognvald* belonging to the North of Scotland, Orkney and Shetland Steam Navigation Company ran aground at full speed in dense fog on the north side of Brough Head, Stronsay. Visibility had been reasonable until the light on North Ronaldsay had been sighted, but had then deteriorated rapidly. Immediately after grounding the vessel listed violently to starboard and remained perched precariously on a reef at the bottom of Brough Head. All seventy passengers were safely landed on Stronsay, some still in their night attire. The *St Rognvald* was carrying a consignment of livestock and, apart from a pony which managed to swim ashore, all of the animals were drowned. Little of the other cargo or mail was salvaged as the wreck slipped off the reef on which she was lying during an easterly gale and sank in deep water just over a week after stranding. The *St Rognvald* does not appear to have been a very lucky ship as nine years previously she had run ashore on the Head of Work near Kirkwall in very similar circumstances, fortunately without suffering major damage.

The only vessel definitely known to have been wrecked on the rocky island of Sule Skerry, lying 50 miles to the west of Stromness, was the Grimsby steam trawler *Sophron* which ran aground in dense fog on 29 September 1902 while returning from the Icelandic fishing grounds. Her crew of ten got ashore safely in the trawler's lifeboat and were given shelter by the lightkeepers before being taken to Stromness by the Grimsby trawler *Uriel*. Another trawler lost in Orkney due to fog was the *Badger* of Aberdeen which was wrecked on the Bow Rock, Westray. She had been returning from twelve days fishing off Iceland and had grounded at two o'clock in the morning of 26 May 1906. Immediately on stranding the *Badger*'s siren was blown and a Grimsby drifter stood by and agreed to assist in helping to refloat the trawler. A kedge was laid out using the trawler's lifeboat, but during the operation this capsized, drowning the mate. Papa Westray Rocket Brigade was called out and put off in the local doctor's boat to try to get a line aboard the trawler but it was extremely difficult for the rocket to be aimed accurately as the boat was pitching violently in the heavy ground swell and it was only at the fifth attempt that a line was got aboard. All eight survivors were then successfully taken off, although one man was washed out of the breeches buoy as he was being hauled to safety, but managed to cling on until he could be rescued.

While outward bound for the fishing grounds the German steam trawler *Kryno Albrecht* of Geestemunde ran aground in fog at full speed on the Rumble Holm off Whalsay on 20 March 1909. The trawler, completely disabled, then floated off and drifted onto the North Heoga Baa. As it was obvious that she would shortly sink the crew of eleven took to their lifeboat and were boarded by two Whalsay men who piloted them to safety. The local boatmen were later rewarded with a gift of money by the German government in recognition of their bravery.

In the case of the 3,467 ton gross *Malin Head* of Belfast, tidal conditions were presumed to have been the cause of the steamer running ashore at Ness of Huna, Caithness on 22 October 1910. She had been on a voyage from the Tees to Montreal with a cargo of pig iron and it seems that her master had underestimated the strength of currents in the Inner Sound between Stroma and Caithness. Two days after going ashore the steamer's back broke, her hull became badly twisted and all compartments were flooded. In spite of this an attempt was made to salvage the ship and she was in fact refloated at the beginning of November, but had to be beached in Gills Bay as she was making so much water. Two men were badly injured during salvage operations when they were struck by a parting tow rope. Fog also caused the loss of the Liverpool-registered *Duna* which ran aground at Old Head, South Ronaldsay in zero visibility on 26 July 1912. She had been bound from Härnosand to Liverpool with a cargo of wood and wood pulp. The nineteen crew and three women passengers abandoned ship in two lifeboats. One was spotted by the trawler *Star of Peace* which landed the passengers and ten crew men at Wick while the other managed to reach the Pentland Skerries and continue to safety the following day when the fog lifted. Nothing was salvaged from the *Duna* which sank in deep water with only the tops of her masts showing.

Shortly after sailing from Grangemouth, with a cargo of coal for her home port of Bergen on 12 January 1913, the Norwegian steamer *Dovre* encountered severe weather in the North Sea, sustained considerable damage and developed a list after the cargo started to shift. On 16 January she sprang a leak in the engine room and, as the pumps were unable to cope, the crew were set to bale with buckets and just managed to keep the water below the level of the fires. Later the same day, while trying to seek shelter from the continuing south-easterly hurricane, the steamer went hard aground on a submerged rock in the mouth of Aith Voe, Bressay. The Aberdeen steam trawler *Morven* put off from Lerwick to try to render assistance and while coming alongside struck the *Dovre* on the starboard side cutting a large hole which caused the engine room to flood completely. With the steamer filling rapidly with water and listing heavily to port, the crew had no choice but to abandon ship and were landed by the *Morven* at Lerwick. Some of the cargo of coal was salvaged before the ship slipped into deeper water and sank.

On 28 June 1914, having landed a consignment of empty casks at the Alexandra whaling station, Colla Firth, the 231 ton Norwegian steamer *Robert Lee* set sail for Liverpool with a general cargo. Visibility rapidly deteriorated and shortly before daybreak the steamer grounded on the Stoura Baa off the north end of Brother Isle in Yell Sound. The ship remained fast in spite of the engines being put full astern. In the very strong tide and heavy swell the ship broached to and developed such a severe list that the feed-pump could not maintain a supply of water to the boilers. The mate was then sent in one of the ship's lifeboats to obtain assistance from the whaling station and shortly afterwards the steamer *Queen Alexandra* arrived to take off as much of the ship's cargo and stores as possible. About 300 bales of stockfish, 350 cases of sardines and a quantity of ship's stores were salvaged but early the next morning the *Robert Lee* filled with water, capsized and sank in deep water. The master and chief engineer, who had stood by the casualty all night, landed safely at Colla Firth, the remainder of the crew having been taken off the previous day.

The mail steamer *St Rognvald* wrecked Brough Head, Stronsay 24 April 1900. (Orkney Library)

5

The First World War

The 17,274 ton gross luxury liner *Oceanic* was the largest ship ever to have been wrecked in the Shetland Islands when she ran aground on the Hoevdi Grund, east of Foula, on 8 September 1914. At the outbreak of hostilities between Britain and Germany on 4 August, the ship was requisitioned by the Admiralty, fitted with 4.7in guns, and commissioned as an armed merchant cruiser. A detachment of naval officers and ratings also joined the ship which was commanded by Captain Slayter RN, although her peacetime master, Captain Smith, remained on board when she was sent to patrol off Shetland and intercept any enemy shipping trying to slip through the British blockade.

Having sailed from Lerwick on 6 September, the ship was to the west of Foula the following evening, zigzagging as an anti-submarine precaution. Due to the divided command and faulty navigation, which put her true position some thirteen miles further north than that estimated by her navigator, the *Oceanic* ran hard aground on the Hoevdi Grund shortly after nine o'clock next morning. Fortunately the sea was calm and all of the ship's complement were taken off by the Aberdeen trawler *Glenogil*. Attempts to refloat the liner were unsuccessful, but all the guns were salvaged before the 685ft ship had broken up and disappeared completely in just over three weeks. The wreck site was relocated in August 1973 and, working over a six year period, the two-man team of Alex Crawford and Simon Martin recovered more than 200 tons of non-ferrous scrap. One of the *Oceanic*'s manganese bronze propeller blades now stands outside the Shetland Museum in Lerwick.

With the outbreak of hostilities in 1914 Scapa Flow became a naval base of the first strategic importance. As it was perceived (with considerable foresight) that submarines would present a major threat to any fleet anchored there, four of the minor entrances adjacent to the North Sea were closed by blockships, a total of twenty-two being sunk in just over a year. Most were old and purchased from ship breakers, like the 3,033 ton net ex-Royal Mail Lines steamer *Thames* obtained from the Forth Ship Breaking Company and scuttled in Kirk Sound in January 1915. Another, the *Urmstone Grange* had stranded in Patagonia and been condemned before being returned to Britain. She was then purchased by the Admiralty and sunk in Burra Sound in September 1914. In all about 50,000 gross tons of shipping were sunk. Some of it was scuttled more or less intact, with permanent fittings still aboard and these provided a rich source of 'bits and pieces' for island households and military camps alike.

The threat that submarines posed to Scapa Flow's early and wholly inadequate defences was shown all too clearly when the *U 18*, commanded by Kapitan Leutenant von Hennig actually managed to enter the anchorage via Hoxa Sound on 23 November 1914. Providentially, all of the main naval units were at sea, with only a few destroyers and trawlers remaining. However, while entering Hoxa Sound the *U 18* had in fact been observed by the examination steamer *Tokio* which raised the alarm. While trying to escape back out to sea it was rammed by HM Trawler *Dorothy Gray*, bending the periscope over at right angles and damaging the hydroplane motor. Without any means of checking his course while submerged, or trimming his ship, von Hennig grounded on the Pentland Skerries while trying to regain the open sea. Realising that there was no chance of escaping he surfaced, ordered the crew to abandon ship and scuttled the submarine. One man was drowned but twenty-six survivors were picked up by the destroyer HMS *Garry*.

Because of stringent wartime censorship regulations, almost all contemporary reports of civilian shipping casualties for this period are at best sketchy and latterly non-existent. In pitch darkness early in the morning of 15 January 1915 the 1,260 gross ton Norwegian steamer *Skotfos*, on a voyage from Trondheim to Manchester with a cargo of wood, woodpulp and carbide, grounded on Seal Skerry,

North Ronaldsay. As the lighthouse on Dennis Ness was extinguished at the time because of wartime regulations, Captain Jorgensen had been unable to obtain an accurate fix at night while trying to make a landfall in Orkney. The ship had gone ashore at high tide so it was possible for the crew to climb over the side at low water and walk to the highest point of the Skerry from where they were rescued by boatmen from North Ronaldsay. Ten days later, after a spell of bad weather, the wreck caught fire and burned for over a week before extinguishing itself. It was then bought by a group of North Ronaldsay men who were able to salvage a very substantial amount of carbide from the burned-out hulk.

Vessels sailing to and from neutral countries on the Continent during the First World War were obliged to pass through British Contraband Control to ensure that no cargoes reached the Central Powers. The Danish steamer *Canadia* was en route from Lerwick to Kirkwall for examination, with a British prize crew on board, when she ran aground on 12 March 1915 in pitch darkness and a heavy swell at Helli Stack on the west side of Fair Isle. As the wreck seemed likely to slip off into deep water at any moment the crew of the wrecked steamer, acting on the shouted advice of the islanders who had arrived on the scene in answer to distress rockets sent up, climbed on to the stack. Due to the heavy sea running it was not possible for the local Lifeboat to get alongside, but with considerable difficulty all the survivors were taken off the stack with the aid of a cliff ladder and ropes. The only casualty was the master whose face and hands had been badly burned by a rocket. The 4,323 ton gross *Canadia* had been on a voyage from Galveston with a cargo of cotton and flour for Göteborg and a considerable amount of the latter was salvaged and consumed locally.

The circumstances surrounding the loss of the 1,441 ton gross Australian barque *Avanti Savoia* on the night of 3–4 April 1915 at Culswick on the west side of Shetland are uncertain as there were no survivors from the crew of seventeen and no one on shore saw her go aground. There was a full gale with a heavy swell running at the time and the wreck broke up completely. The *Avanti Savoia* was 156 days out from Iquique in Chile with a cargo of nitrate for Rotterdam. By a tragic coincidence one of those lost was a local man, Christopher

Fraser, whose home was only three miles from the scene of the disaster. Six of the bodies including that of Fraser were recovered, and buried at Skeld churchyard.

Later the same year, on 12 August, the Stockholm-registered steamer *Kiruna* grounded in dense fog on the Muckle Pentland Skerry while on a voyage from Philadelphia to Stockholm with a cargo of coal. The crew of thirty-five took to the lifeboats next day when it became obvious that the ship was going to become a total loss and landed at Wick. An early oil tanker, the *Llama* (ex *Brilliant*), belonging to the Standard Oil Company of New Jersey, stranded on rocks about half a mile southwest of Skea Skerry, Westray, on 31 October 1915. She had sailed from New York with a cargo of gas oil and was calling at Kirkwall for clearance from Contraband Control before completing the final day of her voyage to Copenhagen. Initially there were hopes that the tanker would be refloated and the captain and seven crew members remained on board, but they had to be taken off when the weather worsened. On 9 November the ship was washed off the reef into deep water with only the top of one mast showing.

The last vessel to be lost in 1915 was the Oslo-registered steel barque *Marco Polo* which went ashore on 6 December at Jack's Reef, Stronsay, in a southeasterly gale while on a voyage from Sweden to Melbourne with a cargo of timber. It was clear from the outset that the barque was a total loss and the day after stranding she was handed over by her captain to the local Receiver of Wrecks. Salvage operations on her cargo continued until the end of the month but were greatly hampered by bad weather. The *Marco Polo* had been built in 1892 by the Grangemouth Dockyard Company and was the last large sailing ship to be lost in Orkney.

During the First World War, the British export trade in coal was continued as far as possible, but on a much reduced scale. The iron-built Swedish steamer *Birka* laden with a cargo of Welsh coal for Göteborg ran aground on the Bow Rock, off the extreme northern end of Westray, late in the evening of 10 January 1916 and broke up almost immediately in the northwesterly gale. There were no survivors and next day five bodies, including that of the captain's wife, were washed ashore along with wreckage and some of the cargo of coal.

By the middle of 1916 the military situation on the Eastern Front had deteriorated so badly, due to a series of successful offensives mounted by the Central Powers, that the British government decided to send Lord Kitchener, the War Minister, to try to bolster the tottering Russian war effort. Kitchener arrived at Scapa Flow on the morning of 5 June and, after conferring with Admiral Jellicoe over lunch, sailed the same afternoon in the cruiser HMS *Hampshire* with an escort of two destroyers. Weather conditions had been deteriorating all day and by the time the squadron weighed anchor it was blowing a full gale. Because of the severe weather it had not been possible to carry out routine mine-sweeping operations either on the usual route up the eastern side of Orkney, or on the more sheltered westerly route which the *Hampshire* decided to take, a fatal decision because a week earlier the *U 75* had laid a field of thirty-four mines just off Birsay Bay.

After clearing Hoy Sound the *Hampshire*'s C.O. ordered the escorting destroyers back to Scapa Flow because they were unable to keep up in the severe weather. Shortly before eight o'clock, when she was about two miles off Marwick Head, the cruiser struck two mines and sank in less than fifteen minutes. Lord Kitchener was last seen in the gun-room flat in the company of a naval officer. It was not possible to launch any lifeboats because of the very heavy seas and only twelve men reached the shore alive. Over 650 men were lost and none of Lord Kitchener's party survived. Because of the massive surf it was not possible for boats to put off from the Birsay shore and rescue survivors.

An eyewitness to the sinking, Sub-Lieutenant J. Spence, who was at home in Birsay on sick leave at the time, wrote a report on the sinking ten months after the event, no one having taken the trouble to inverview any potential witnesses. In his report the Sub-Lieutenant stated that, when it was realised that the cruiser was in trouble, a telegram was immediately dispatched to the naval authorities, but was quite categorical in saying that no rescue ships had reached the area by midnight. There therefore appears to have been a disastrous series of failures by the naval authorities on three counts:

1 A failure to appreciate that Germany had ocean-going mine-laying

submarines, operating in that area.

2 A failure to use intelligence provided by the code-breaking operation of Room 40 which reported the presence of *U 75* off Orkney with orders to lay mines off the west of Orkney.

3 The total failure to mount a rescue operation at sea which, if carried out expeditiously, could have saved hundreds of lives. This last omission caused great offence in Orkney as the Stromness Lifeboat with the local expertise of its crew could have rendered priceless service that night had it been summoned.

Due to the catastrophic effects of the German submarine offensive on unconvoyed Allied shipping, rigorous censorship was imposed and the publication of all casualty reports were suppressed from the beginning of 1917 till the end of hostilities in November 1918. For example the Swedish steamer *Scandinavic* of Gothenburg went ashore in unknown circumstances on Skea Skerry, Westray on 1 February 1917. The steamer, which was homeward bound with a cargo of cotton from Galveston, apparently broke up and became a total loss after a week and that is all that is officially known about the loss of the *Scandinavic*.

Surprisingly, it was not until March 1917 that the first major war casualty due to enemy action occurred in the waters around Shetland. The British submarine *E 49* sailed from Balta Sound, Unst, on 12 March to patrol off Muckle Flugga. Shortly after midday, while between the islands of Balta and Huney, the submarine struck a mine which blew off her bows and she sank with the loss of all hands. Three months later, on 30 June 1917, the destroyer HMS *Cheerful* sank after striking a mine off Helli Ness, Cunningsburgh, with only eighteen survivors from her complement of sixty officers and men. In 1926 the Lerwick boat *Isabella Gordon* brought up part of one of the destroyer's lifeboats with the brass letter C still attached.

In 9 July 1917, shortly after eleven o'clock in the evening, the battleship HMS *Vanguard* was blown apart by a huge internal explosion while moored off the island of Flotta in Scapa Flow. Debris was scattered over a huge area, but incredibly caused no other casualties. Three survivors were picked up, but one, a lieutenant commander, died next day. This brought the total dead to 804 men, including a Commander Ito, an observer from the Imperial Japanese Navy. The subsequent Court of Inquiry concluded that the explosion had been due to the spontaneous detonation of unstable cordite. Cordite, the propellant used in large calibre naval guns, was normally stored in the magazine in silk bags which had no resistance to 'flash' should spontaneous combustion take place in any of the adjacent charges. This problem had been recognised by the Germans, who stored and used their cordite in thin-walled brass canisters which had excellent 'flash' resistance. Two other British warships had been lost in similar circumstances, HMS *Bulwark* at Sheerness in 1914 and HMS *Natal* at Cromarty in 1915. Limited salvage operations on the wreck were undertaken in 1957 to recover non-ferrous scrap and armour plate. Since then the naval authorities have decided that the site should be considered as a war grave.

In the autumn of 1917 Allied and neutral shipping suffered a series of disastrous losses off Bressay when the German submarine *UC 40* sank or damaged a total of seven vessels either by mine or torpedo. On 10 September the 1,316 ton Swansea-registered steamer *Parkmill*, with a cargo of coal for Harstad, was sunk by a mine off Kirkabister lighthouse, Bressay. Two days later on 12 September HM Trawler *Asia* was also sunk by a mine off Bressay. There was some redress in the balance on 29 September when the *UC 55* lost trim while laying mines off Helli Ness, Cunningsburgh. In order to prevent the submarine from sinking uncontrollably to the bottom all tanks were blown and it was abandoned and scuttled as soon as it reached surface, shortly before two British destroyers arrived on the scene. Ten men were lost from her complement of twenty-six.

The Russian steamer *Slavonic* (ex *Teutonic*) was torpedoed by the *UC 40* on 19 October, six cables south southwest of Bard Head while inward bound from Archangel to Lerwick. Although she was taken in tow the steamer sank thirty minutes later. On 21 October the 808 ton Copenhagen-registered steamer *Anglo-Dane* in an eastbound convoy for Norway was either sunk by a mine or torpedoed just off Kirkabister lighthouse. The ship was an old one, having been built of iron at Newcastle in 1866, and had a cargo of coal for Elsinore. Later the same day in almost exactly identical circumstances the Danish steamer *Flyderborg*, in a westbound convoy from Norway, was sunk off the Bard of Bressay. The third casualty that day was the London-registered *Novington*, also torpedoed off the Bard of Bressay. Her crew abandoned ship and she drifted ashore on the east side of Bressay. Although badly damaged she was subsequently refloated and repaired. Finally on 24 October the *UC 40* torpedoed and sank the Russian steamer *Woron* just off the southern entrance to Bressay Sound. Thus, in the space of six weeks, over 13,000 tons of shipping had been sunk or damaged by enemy action off Shetland.

A month later, on 24 November 1917, the Dundee-registered steamer *Glenisla* with a cargo of coal for Slimstad, sank in the main fairway between Bressay and Ness of Sound after colliding with the *Glenelg*. The crew of twenty-three were all picked up. Casualties continued when the 1,968 ton gross *Waterville* of Leith was stranded and wrecked in Brei Wick, just south of Lerwick, on 26 November 1917. She had been bound from Archangel with a cargo of flax and must have been one of the last British ships to have left Russia, then in the throes of the Communist revolution. Her crew of twenty-three and one passenger were all landed safely. On 12 December the Plymouth-registered trawler *Amadavat*, 171 ton gross, sank off the eastern side of Shetland, possibly in the vicinity of Bressay, after striking a mine with the loss of her skipper and eight men. On the same day the Glasgow-registered *Leonatus* in an eastbound convoy for Bergen was also sunk by a mine off Bard Head. Finally, early in the following year, on 2 January 1918, the steamer *Gwladmena* of Liverpool with a cargo of coal for Lerwick sank on the southwest side of Brei Wick after colliding with the *Flora*, but her crew of twenty-two were all saved.

While returning from patrol off the east coast of Orkney the two M Class destroyers, HMS *Narborough* and HMS *Opal*, ran aground in a blizzard and pitch dark night at Clett of Crura, South Ronaldsay, on 12 January 1918. There was only one survivor, an able seaman, from the combined ships' companies of 180 officers and men. That anyone should have survived in the terrible conditions was incredible – the unfortunate man was not discovered until thirty-six hours after the stranding, huddled for shelter on a narrow cliff ledge. The Court of Inquiry decided that in shaping his course the commander of HMS *Opal*, the lead destroyer, had either not made sufficient allowance for northerly drift or made a small but disastrous error in his course. During 1932 the propellers and some of the larger items of scrap were salvaged from the wrecks.

The last warship to be lost in the area during the First World War was the German submarine *UB 116*, sunk by controlled mine off Pan Hope, Flotta on 28 October 1918. Her commander had been ordered to try to enter Scapa Flow via Hoxa Sound and sink as many ships as possible, German intelligence believing, quite incredibly, that it was unprotected by either mines or boom nets. In the event they were disastrously wrong and as soon as the submarine tried to enter the sound on the evening of 28 October her motors were heard on hydrophones and all defences alerted. Shortly before midnight she was located precisely on a detector loop and blown up by a controlled mine. Next day, with oil and air bubbles still rising from the wreck, depth charges were dropped and they brought up a German naval watch coat. There were no survivors. Apparently part of the submarine's conning tower was salvaged a few weeks later and displayed at St Margaret's Hope in South Ronaldsay.

The Wick schooner *Isabella*, 95 ton net, on a voyage from Sunderland to Stromness with a cargo of coal was seen leaving Sinclair Bay, Caithness on 1 November 1918. Nothing more was heard of her or her crew of four, but an unidentified body was washed ashore at John o'Groats later in the month and it is presumed that the *Isabella* had foundered in heavy weather off Duncansby Head.

Salvage operation on the Aberdeen trawler *Ben Namur* wrecked at the Bay of Skaill, Orkney 10 October 1920. It also provides a convenient fishing platform for the local 'loons'. (Orkney Library)

Scapa Flow, 21 June 1919. German sailors pull away from the scuttled battleship *Bayern* towards an unpleasant welcome from the Royal Navy. A photograph taken by the war artist Bernard Gribble. (Maritime Museum, Poole)

6

The Sunken Fleet

All previous shipping losses in Orkney and Shetland fade into insignificance when compared with the huge tonnage sunk in the scuttling of the German High Seas Fleet at Scapa Flow on 21 June 1919. Under the terms of the Armistice of 11 November 1918 the Germans were required to hand over for internment seventy-four warships, namely ten battleships, six battlecruisers, eight light cruisers and fifty destroyers. Originally, the British and French Admiralties had demanded that the ships be surrendered outright, but it was eventually agreed that they should be interned in neutral ports, or failing that, Allied ports. As understandably no neutral country wished to be saddled with such problems and responsibilities it was decided in the end that the seventy-four German warships should be interned in Scapa Flow under the supervision of the Royal Navy.

The Internment Formation, under the command of Admiral Ludwig von Reuter, sailed from Wilhelmshaven on 19 November 1918 and anchored in the Firth of Forth where all ships were searched before being dispatched in groups to Scapa Flow. In the Flow the German battleships, battlecruisers and light cruisers were anchored to the west, north and east of Cava, with the destroyers lying off Hoy in Gutter Sound. The last ship to arrive, on 9 January 1919, was the 28,060 ton *Baden* the largest type of battleship in the Imperial German Navy, a replacement for the incomplete *Mackensen*.

Peace negotiations between the Allies and Germany dragged on until 6 May 1919, when the draft treaty was handed to the Germans.

To the German navy the terms seemed exceptionally harsh, involving the enforced handover of all the interned ships together with another fifty-two destroyers. It was then that Admiral von Reuter decided (independently of Berlin so far as can be discovered) to go ahead with the scuttling of the High Seas Fleet to prevent it from falling into the hands of the Allies. Final peace negotiations continued until the middle of June when Germany was presented with an ultimatum of either accepting the conditions or resuming hostilities on 21 June. Admiral von Reuter only learned of the ultimatum on 20 June from an out-of-date copy of *The Times* and immediately gave orders for the scuttling to take place next day. Entirely unknown to him a two day extension was made to the ultimatum at the last minute.

Incredibly, on the morning of 21 June the British First Battle Squadron, under the command of Admiral Sir Sidney Freemantle, steamed out of Scapa Flow for exercises in the Pentland Firth, leaving the German High Seas Fleet virtually unguarded except for a couple of destroyers. Aboard the German ships all measures for scuttling were complete and at 10.30am the coded flag signal for scuttling was given. The first ship to go down was the battleship *Friedrich der Grosse* which capsized and sank at 12.16pm with battleships, cruisers and destroyers following at regular intervals. Scapa Flow was soon a chaotic mass of sinking ships, wreckage, oil and lifeboats crammed with German sailors.

A water-tender, the *Flying Kestrel*, with a party of four hundred Stromness school children aboard on a special excursion trip round the High Seas Fleet, found itself in the middle of this shambles. Amongst those on board were the late Mr and Mrs William Groundwater, then pupils of Stromness Higher Grade School, whose taped reminiscences are preserved in Orkney Library Sound Archives.

William Groundwater: It began to be realised that ships were getting low in the water and were sinking. There was lots of activity with [German] sailors dragging boats and some dragging rafts and throwing them overboard. British destroyers began to steam round and sailors started to jump down into rafts from German ships. Like a slow motion picture the ships began to sink and to turn turtle and some went down by the stern, all on board [the *Flying Kestrel*] were speechless with excitement.

Rosetta Groundwater: The *Flying Kestrel* was ordered back to the depot ship and as we arrived I distinctly saw the *Seydlitz* turn turtle with water come streaming out of the seacocks. I definitely saw one man shot and he dropped right off the stern of the boat, other men were standing with their hands up . . . To us it just seemed to have to be an adventure story we had been reading . . . we just thought it was put on, probably for our benefit as school children.

Another eyewitness to these extraordinary events was James Wilson of Graemsay who was with his father 'at the creels' off the Holm of Houton at the time of the scuttling:

'It was a beautiful summer day, calm with a little wind. We had recently been allowed back into the Flow, which had been closed during the war, to resume lobster fishing. Suddenly, some time about midday, the German Fleet began to sink with a huge rushing, roaring noise. As the boats went down they threw up huge spouts of water and foam and when they were gone the sea was littered with wreckage, wood, lifeboats and oil. In the distance shots could be heard and we learned later that several German sailors had been killed.

By the time Admiral Freemantle's squadron had raced back to Scapa Flow on receiving news of the scuttling it was too late as most of the larger German ships were beyond assistance. In the event one battleship, the *Baden*, three cruisers, the *Frankfurt, Emden* and the *Nurnberg*, and a few destroyers were beached. It was also painfully obvious that, during the scuttling, the British officers remaining in Scapa Flow had panicked and ordered indiscriminate shooting at the sinking ships and their crews with small arms and automatic weapons. A total of eight Germans were killed and a further sixteen wounded by gunfire. Next day a ninth German sailor was shot and killed aboard a British battleship in unexplained circumstances. The German casualties were buried at Lyness Naval Cemetery on Hoy.

The final total of warships sunk was ten battleships, five battle-cruisers and thirty-two destroyers, in all some 430,000 tons of shipping. Given the massive technical problems involved in raising the scuttled ships there seemed little likelihood of any of them ever being removed, but in 1922, after considerable problems and delays, a syndicate of Stromness businessmen succeeded in raising the destroyer *G 89* and towing it to Stromness for breaking up. The condenser tubes were cut up and sold off locally as curtain rails. By the end of 1924 another four destroyers had been raised by the Lerwick-based Scapa Flow Salvage and Shipbreaking Company.

It was also during 1924 that Ernest Cox of the shipbreaking firm of Cox and Danks started operations, having purchased outright or obtained options on the rest of the sunken fleet. With no salvage expertise he set about purchasing suitable equipment and hiring staff to undertake this huge operation, setting up headquarters in the more or less abandoned naval base at Lyness. Apart from skilled workers such as divers and artificers, the labour force was hired locally, which helped to mitigate the worst effects of the severe economic problems of the 1920s and 1930s.

Work was first concentrated on salvaging destroyers which were raised using an ex-German floating dock cut longitudinally into two parts. At low water the two sections of dock were positioned on either side of the sunken ship, chains, or latterly massive steel cables, passed under the hull and both ends made fast to the docks. When the tide rose giving an average lift of about seven feet, the dock sections acted as pontoons and the wreck was lifted off the bottom in its cradle of chains or cables. The chains initially used for this operation proved quite inadequate for the job, they snapped and whipped alarmingly, fortunately without any being killed, and were therefore replaced by stronger steel cables. The dock, with the destroyer suspended underneath, was then towed towards the shore until it grounded. At low water the cables were then shortened and the whole process repeated until the destroyer was sufficiently clear of the surface for it to be patched, pumped out and refloated. On average it was possible for Cox to raise one destroyer per month, but with favourable circumstances the *S 65* was refloated in four days. Once raised the destroyers were either scrapped locally or towed south to be broken up.

In all twenty-four destroyers were raised before efforts were turned to the massive capital ships, the first of which was the 26,947 ton battlecruiser *Hindenburg*. She had sunk more or less upright, with her bridge, funnels and guns above water, making her the most prominent feature of the Scapa Flow seascape. After a detailed divers' survey it was found that over eight hundred holes would have to be sealed, the biggest of which required a huge wooden patch, this being to cover the hole left when a rusted funnel had to be removed. Cox intended refloating the *Hindenburg* upright by pumping her out and using four sections of floating dock to help with buoyancy until she was beached. In all it took five months to plug all the holes, but attempts to raise the battlecruiser failed due to a combination of lack of transverse stability and bad weather.

Work on the *Hindenburg* was abandoned at the beginning of September 1926 and salvage operations were started on the capsized battlecruiser *Moltke*, lying in seventy feet of water between Rysa Little and Cava. As she was completely submerged even at low tide a different approach was required. Essentially the hull had to be sealed and pumped full of compressed air, which would allow the scuttled battlecruiser to float to the surface. In reality there were horrendous technical problems, not the least of which was the provision of unrestricted and pressure tight access to the sunken ship. This was solved by fabricating sets of air trunking of suitable length, complete with airlocks and ladders, out of old boilers and bolting the bottom of them to the upturned bottom of the *Moltke*. It was then possible to pump out the trunking, burn access manholes through the hull plating and start filling the upturned hull with compressed air. Salvage workers were then able to enter the hull and start work on sealing it into a series of watertight compartments so that longitudinal and transverse stability could be controlled. Inside the ship all necessary watertight doors had to be closed and pipes cut and blanked off at bulkheads. This was in addition to plugging all the portholes, condenser inlets and so on in the hull.

After ten months of filthy, back-breaking work the hull and compartments had been sealed and the 22,979 ton *Moltke* was raised (not without several last minute hitches) amid a mass of foam, mud and fountains of water as surplus compressed air escaped. She was then towed to Lyness, beached, and over 3,000 tons of metal stripped from her interior. In May 1929, with the airlock trunking cut down or removed and a compressor hut and a bunk house bolted to the upturned hull, the *Moltke* was towed south to Rosyth for breaking up. A severe southerly gale was encountered en route which drove the whole procession of three tugs and the upturned battlecruiser back towards Scapa Flow before moderating. Having nearly collided with the Forth Bridge when two pilots (one civilian and one naval) failed to agree on a course, the *Moltke* was safely berthed in the naval dry dock at Rosyth.

The method of raising the *Moltke* was used, with minor variations, on all the sunken capital ships to be raised apart from the *Hindenburg*. In 1928 Cox made an ill-starred attempt to raise the capsized battlecruiser *Seydlitz* on her side. This ended in disaster when a patch failed and she capsized completely and sank, fortunately without causing any casualties. The *Hindenburg* was eventually raised upright in July 1930 after the stability problems were finally overcome.

Although the firm had salvaged some 170,000 tons of shipping, operations had not been profitable and in 1932, with a collapse in scrap prices, Ernest Cox sold out completely to the newly-formed firm of Metal Industries. With the improved financial control, new equipment and a sudden unexpected upturn in scrap prices the new undertaking proved immensely profitable and a total of six capital ships were raised using the airlock technique. Considering the technical difficulties, most of the operations were remarkably free of problems. However, in January 1933 the battleship *Bayern* made an uncontrolled and unscheduled ascent which was so violent that all four heavy gun turrets were torn off and fell to the bottom of Scapa Flow off Houton, where they lie to this day.

The last ship to be raised was the battlecruiser *Derfflinger* which was finally brought to the surface in August 1939, on the eve of the Second World War. She spent the entire war moored off Rysa Little with a small team of fitters on board the upturned hull maintaining pressure and trim. Finally in 1946, after being loaded inside an ex-Royal Navy floating dock, she was towed to Faslane on the Firth of Clyde and broken up. Three battleships, the *König*, *Markgraf* and *Kronprinz Wilhelm*, and the light cruisers *Cöln*, *Dresden*, *Brummer* and *Karlsruhe* were considered to be lying at too great a depth for economic salvage and still lie on the bottom of Scapa Flow off Cava. In the post-war period salvage operations, principally by Nundy Metal Industries Limited, have been confined to the piecemeal removal of non-ferrous scrap. Today the seven scuttled warships are a major source of attraction for the two thousand subaqua divers who now visit Scapa Flow every year.

Salvage operations underway on the battlecruiser *Seydlitz* scuttled in Scapa Flow on 21 June 1919. Probably taken in 1929 after an attempt to raise the battlecruiser sideways had failed. (Sandy Tait, Stromness)

The Moor Line steamer *Linkmoor* almost completely high and dry at Scarfskerry, Caithness, 10 November 1930. (Sutherland Manson, Thurso)

The capsized and derelict Danish three-masted schooner *Martin Nisson* driven ashore at Scousborough, Dunrossness, Shetland, 30 December 1929. (Shetland Museum)

7

Inter-War Years

Of all the different classes of shipping lost in the waters around Orkney and Shetland during the inter-war years, by far the worst to suffer were trawlers. A total of seventy-eight lives were lost in twenty-eight incidents, with the majority of casualties occurring down Orkney's west coast from the Brough of Birsay southwards to Tor Ness in Hoy. In the days before sophisticated electronic navigational aids this stretch of coast all too often proved a death trap to trawlers, especially in poor visibility and heavy weather. Anyone who has ventured onto the cliff tops at Yesnaby during a westerly gale will have seen a band of tumbling white water and surf extending several hundred yards to seaward from the cliff base. Even the best-founded vessel stranded in such conditions would be smashed to pieces in a few minutes, with near-certain death the fate for its unfortunate crew.

The first trawler to be lost after the First World War was the *Ben Namur* of Aberdeen which stranded on the north side of the Bay of Skaill on 10 October 1920. There was dense fog at the time with a heavy ground swell running and two of the crew were washed overboard and drowned when the trawler struck. The survivors managed to float a line ashore and were all brought to safety before Stromness Rocket Brigade arrived. A subsequent Board of Trade Inquiry found that the skipper had failed to establish his position before setting a course which led to the stranding of his ship and his certificate was suspended for nine months.

After the end of hostilities in 1918 the herring industry in Shetland temporarily revived, but on a reduced scale due to smaller catches and the loss of traditional export markets, but there was sufficient business to employ the service of some carriers. One of those, the Swedish steamer *Jane* of Gothenburg sailed from the fishing station at Balta Sound in Unst with a cargo of herring on 19 July 1923 and ran aground on Linga at the southern entrance to Bluemull Sound between Yell and Unst. Shortly afterwards she floated off on the flood tide before going ashore again on Sound Grunay and sinking in ten fathoms of water. The crew of fourteen which included two women, a stewardess and a cook, were picked up safely.

The German barque *Bohus* (ex. *Bertha*), a training ship for the German merchant marine which also carried commercial cargoes, sailed from Gothenburg on 23 April 1924 in ballast, bound for Taltal in Chile with a crew of thirty-eight and one stowaway. Due to bad weather the master, Captain Blume, was unable to take any astronomical sights after leaving Sweden and by 27 April the barque was some sixty miles further north than the estimated position. Disastrously, in the continuing bad visibility which was less than one mile, the captain mistook the light on Out Skerries for that on Fair Isle and at two o'clock in the afternoon of 27 April the barque was embayed in Otters Wick on the east side of Yell. An anchor was dropped but the cable parted in the strong south-southeast wind and the *Bohus* drove ashore at Ness of Quheyin on the north side of the bay. As it was obvious that the ship was about to break up and slip into deep water, the crew abandoned ship and four men were lost. One, Cadet Tom Ebert, saved four of his fellow cadets before being washed off a rock and drowned. Three bodies were recovered and buried at Mid Yell, their graves being marked by an imposing black granite headstone. As another memorial to those lost the figurehead from the *Bohus* was recovered from the wreck and erected on the Ness of Quheyin where it still remains.

More unusual at that date was a sailing casualty, the four-masted schooner *Kathleen Annie* of London which stranded on the Green Holms, Eday on 29 September 1924. Captained by Commander Worsley of Antarctic fame, she was on passage from Bremen to Newfoundland with a cargo of 17,000 cases of rectified spirit. Attempts to salvage her led to a further loss when the steam drifter *Busy Bee* took on board some of the *Kathleen Annie*'s cargo. This leaked and the alcohol fumes were ignited by cinders from the stoke hold. This resulted in the drifter catching fire and sinking. The schooner was refloated and beached at Kirkwall where the balance of the cargo was salvaged. As she was too badly damaged to be worth repairing the *Kathleen Annie* was broken up. Most of the cargo was recovered but some, as the Lloyd's Casualty Report of the day put it, 'escaped', to be consumed by some of the thirstier islanders who used it to lace their home-brewed ale to give it a bit more 'bite'. Before trying this cocktail one party fed a spoonful to the household cat which expired abruptly! It would seem that the *Kathleen Annie*'s true destination was the United States, then in the throes of Prohibition, and that her cargo would have been turned into bootleg liquor.

The 2,559 ton net Norwegian steamer *Hastings County* ran aground on Auskerry in dense fog on 13 June 1926 while trying to make the Fair Isle passage. She was on a voyage from Hamburg to Montreal with a general cargo which included two motor launches, rum and a consignment of toys. The crew of forty were rescued, thirty-one of them being taken off by the Stromness lifeboat *John A. Hay*. Fortunately the weather remained settled and allowed the salvage of most of the cargo. At the end of September the wreck caught fire, presumably due to spontaneous combustion in the wet bunker coal, and she broke up completely in a southeast gale early in November. All that can be seen today are the remains of the engines lying at high water mark on the rocky shores of Auskerry.

The last pure sailing vessel to be wrecked in Orkney was the local schooner *Mary Grace* of Flotta which stranded on Swona on 27 June 1927 while bound from the Firth of Forth to Kirkwall with a cargo of coal. Fortunately the loss of this survivor from a bygone age ended with the crew escaping ashore in the ship's small boat.

The earliest motor vessel to be wrecked in Shetland was the twin screw *Ustetind* of Älesund which dragged her anchors on Christmas Day 1929 and went to pieces at Silwick in Walls. Earlier that day she had lost one of her propellers and been partially disabled in a southerly storm. The Walls Rocket Brigade managed to fire a line aboard in blizzard conditions and the crew of eleven were all ferried ashore in two trips using the ship's lifeboat. Built in Dramen in 1922 the *Ustetind* had been on a voyage to the Tyne with a cargo of tele-graph poles. Four days later on 29 December the Danish three-masted schooner *Martin Nisson* of Svenborg was swept ashore derelict at Coubal, Scousborough. There was no sign of her crew and the identity of the wreck was only established with difficulty. She had sailed from Sundsvall on 11 November with a cargo of battens for Stornoway. The wreck rapidly broke up and by the middle of January her cargo of wood was coming ashore at points as far apart as the Out Skerries and Fair Isle.

One of the most tragic incidents was the loss of the 155 ton gross steam trawler *Ben Doran* of Aberdeen which went ashore on the Ve Skerries on 28 March 1930. The wreck was not seen from the shore and it was not reported until next day when the Aberdeen trawler *Braconbush* put into Hillswick with the news that survivors had been sighted clinging to the rigging. A full-scale rescue operation was mounted with the nearest Life-saving company being summoned from Lerwick. As they could not reach Hillswick till after dark no rescue attempt by them was possible until early next morning, when the Burra boat *Smiling Morn* had also arrived on the scene. By this time the weather had worsened considerably with a full gale blowing and sleet and snow showers. The Ve Skerries were surrounded by confused breaking seas which made it impossible to close the *Ben Doran* sufficiently to pass a line aboard to the survivors, who could still be seen clinging to the rigging. The trawler's bridge had broken loose and lay over the trawl winch. At that time no lifeboats were stationed in Shetland and the nearest one was summoned from Stromness 120 miles away. When she arrived at the Ve Skerries next day it was found that the *Ben Doran* had broken up and there was no sign of any survivors. As a direct result of the tragedy a lighted buoy with a wave operated whistle was positioned near the Skerries. Later that year the Royal National Lifeboat Institution stationed a lifeboat at Lerwick and in 1933 established another at Aith.

On 10 April 1930, with the Ve Skerries' disaster still fresh in their minds, the inhabitants of Shetland were stunned to learn of the stranding of the mail steamer *St Sunniva* in dense fog on the island of Mousa. In a special edition, *The Shetland News* reported that the steamer had run ashore at about 3.40am on the eastern side of the island while on her scheduled run from Kirkwall to Lerwick. As the stranded vessel was being severely pounded by the ground swell the order to abandon ship was given immediately and the crew and forty or so passengers reached dry land on Mousa safely in the ship's lifeboats. The engine-room staff had had an extremely narrow escape when some of the machinery was driven violently inboard by the force of the stranding and the stokehold had flooded rapidly. While the captain made for Sandlodge on the mainland to raise the alarm, the survivors managed to shelter in a shepherd's bothy. It was not until later that morning that those on Mousa were taken off and landed at Lerwick, most still being in their night attire and having saved little of their personal possessions and luggage. In the event very little was salvaged from the wreck which broke up completely in a southeasterly gale later in the month. A considerable amount of mail was lost and this contained payments to the value of several thousand pounds for knitwear workers in the form of postal orders and drafts for which no compensation could be obtained.

Later the same year, early in the morning of 10 November, the London-registered steamer *Linkmoor* was driven ashore at Scarfskerry, Caithness, after her anchor cables parted in a northerly gale. Due to the prompt action of the Scarfskerry Life-saving company all the steamer's crew were safely brought ashore a little over an hour after the ship had first stranded. The *Linkmoor* had been bound from Liverpool to Blyth in ballast for repairs, having grounded the previous month in Norway. She had anchored to wait for the tide before completing her transit of the Pentland Firth. With continuing bad weather the stranded steamer suffered major damage and after a week the salvors abandoned the case and returned to Leith. As the wreck completely blocked the little harbour at Scarfskerry the bow section had to be blasted apart to allow it to be reopened.

While on a voyage from Leningrad to Belfast with a cargo of wood, the Norwegian steamer *Borg* struck the North Shoal, a submerged reef about ten miles north of the Brough of Birsay on 3 July 1931. By great good fortune the steamer stayed afloat and was able to limp into Birsay Bay where she was beached. The wreck was bought by a syndicate of local business men who managed to salvage a considerable amount of the cargo which was rafted round to Stromness, but the ship itself became a total loss. She became a major local attraction with hundreds of sightseers thronging the beach at Birsay.

Less than a month later, on 26 July, the 3,759 ton Copenhagen-registered steamer *Pennsylvania* stranded in thick fog on Swona. Shortly after sailing from New York with a general cargo the ship had encountered thick weather which had lasted all the way across the Atlantic and the captain had been on the bridge of his ship for ninety-three consecutive hours prior to the stranding. After refusing assistance from the Longhope lifeboat which stood by the casualty, the crew of thirty-three landed on Swona next day in their own boats. Within a week the ship's back had broken and efforts were then concentrated on salvaging the cargo. Later, after the vessel had broken up completely, a substantial amount of the cargo turned up in Caithness and Orkney although how typewriters managed to float or American cigarettes reach shore bone-dry no doubt exercised the minds of the local Customs and Excise officers! Old habits died hard and the *Orcadian* carried a lengthy article on the activities of the 'pirates'.

At exactly the same spot four years later, on 19 August 1935, the Swedish motor ship *Gunnaren* was also stranded in thick fog while on passage from New York to Gothenburg with mails and a general cargo. She was a modern vessel, having been built in Gothenburg in 1930, and reports at the time of her stranding speak of her luxurious and well-found appearance. With her bow stuck fast it was decided to cut the ship in two and tow away the stern section which was still afloat and undamaged. The hull had in fact been more or less cut through when a heavy ground swell got up, causing the tow ropes connected to the salvage tugs to part and the crew remaining on board to abandon ship. At this point the stern broke away from the bows and the cable of a kedge anchor laid out immediately after the stranding also parted. The stern section then finally and permanently drifted ashore about a quarter of a mile from the bow. (By a stroke of great good fortune this extraordinary event was photographed by Mr Tom Rosie who lived on Swona and is shown on pages 142–3.) Salvage operations yielded a large quantity of apples and pears which were sold locally. For their efforts the salvage workers, mostly from Stroma, were paid the somewhat unprincely sum of a shilling an hour.

Little is known about the circumstances surrounding the loss of the 195 ton Granton steam trawler *May Island* which was lost with her crew of ten on Unst, during a violent southeasterly gale in February 1936. Early in the morning of 18 February people living at Norwick on the east side of the island heard a ship's siren being blown. A brief and, as it turned out, incorrect radio message 'Ashore Flugga Rocks' was also picked up. Later in the day large amounts of wreckage and fishing gear were driven ashore at Norwick and next day the tops of two masts were seen off the south side of Lamba Ness. There was no sign of any survivors.

By considerable good fortune none of the previous cargo ships wrecked in the Pentland Firth had been attended by any loss of life, but the grounding of the Finnish motor vessel *Johanna Thorden* of Bradö on 12 January 1937 took a considerable toll. She had gone ashore in poor visibility in a southeasterly gale on the Tarf Tail, Swona shortly after six o'clock in the morning while returning from her maiden voyage to New York with a general cargo for Gothenburg. The violence of the grounding had put the radio out of action and it was impossible to send out a distress call. By superb seamanship two lifeboats carrying thirty-eight passengers and crew managed to leave the ship safely, but one of them was overturned. All those in it perished and the waterlogged boat, containing two bodies, was washed ashore at Dingieshowe, Deerness next day. The other, commanded by the captain, reached South Ronaldsay safely, but capsized in the surf off Kirkhouse Point and only eight people managed to reach the shore alive. It was only at this point that the alarm was raised and a full-scale rescue operation mounted, but no further survivors were found. The thirty persons lost included two women and two children. As recently as the spring of 1986 a quantity of paraffin wax, believed to have come from the *Johanna Thorden*, came ashore in Orkney's east mainland, but nothing else of the cargo, which included several hundred tons of high grade copper, was ever salvaged.

Just over a year later, on 27 January 1938, the Grimsby steam trawler *Leicestershire*, homeward bound from the Icelandic fishing grounds, stranded and went to pieces in thick weather at the Berry, Hoy. The location, remote from any habitation, meant that the first indication of the disaster came when bodies and wreckage were

washed up on Melsetter Links a few days later. There were no survivors from the crew of fifteen and it was not until about a month later
that the trawler's engines and boilers, all that remained, were finally
discovered by lobster fishermen at the Kist, a square slab of rock
lying a few hundred yards off the Berry.

When in 1939 war between Britain and Germany seemed immin-
ent, measures were put in hand to reclose the four minor eastern
entrances of Scapa Flow with blockships as an anti-submarine precaution. By the time war was declared on 3 September only two ships
had in fact been sunk, the concrete barge *Naja* and the Uruguayan
steamer *Seriano* (ex *Evansville*, ex *Lake Tahoe*, ex *SNA4*). As salvage
operations in the inter-war years had removed or blasted flat a signifi-
cant number of the previous blockships, which had also been displaced by the very strong tides, this proved to be a disastrously
inadequate defence.

The Norwegian steamer *Borg* beached at Birsay Bay, Orkney,
3 July 1931 after striking the North Shoal. (Orkney Library)

"St Sunniva" on Mousa.

The mail steamer *St Sunniva* wrecked on Mousa, Shetland 10 April 1930. (Shetland Museum)

8

Second World War
And After

Of all the casualties which occurred in the area during two world
wars, the torpedoing of the battleship HMS *Royal Oak* at Scapa Flow
on 14 October 1939 was the most momentous and its most tragic. It
was momentous for the loss of such a large capital ship and for the
death of over seven hundred of her complement, and it was tragic
because it was entirely avoidable. In spite of the increasing belliger-
ence of the Third Reich and the growing certainty of war and notwithstanding Admiralty pleas, HM Treasury refused to sanction the
release of funds to purchase replacement blockships in Scapa Flow's
four eastern entrances for those that had been removed, blown up or
broken up through the action of time and weather. Those remaining
still presented a formidable hazard to any ship trying to enter Scapa
Flow but not sufficient to deter a resolute, brave and skilful U-boat
captain. Thus it was possible for the *U47* under the command of
Kapitan Leutenant Prien, to slip through a gap in the Kirk Sound
blockships on the night of 13–14th October 1939, fire four torpedoes,
two of which sank HMS *Royal Oak*, and slip back out to the North
Sea entirely undetected. It was only by the mercy of providence that
the rest of the British Home Fleet was at sea, otherwise the conse-
quences might have been even more catastrophic.

As those on board HMS *Royal Oak* did not appreciate what was
happening, even after an early torpedo hit had damaged her stem,
most of the ship's company was below in the mess decks when the
second salvo struck. The resultant explosions caused the ship to cap-
size and sink in less than fifteen minutes with the loss of 786 officers

and men. Although in fairly shallow water, no attempt was made at salvage beyond removing the four propellers. Today her last resting place is marked by a green wreck buoy and a thin slick of oil which still rises to the surface.

With the sinking of HMS *Royal Oak*, frantic efforts were made to seal the four eastern entrances and a total of nineteen blockships were sunk in addition to the two already in position. They were an extraordinarily mixed bag and included a German prize the *Morea* renamed the *Empire Seaman*, a Great Lakes steamer the *Collingdoc* mined off Southend in 1941, and the bows of the motor tanker *Inverlane* mined off the Tyne in 1939. To provide permanent protection, causeways were built on the express orders of the then First Lord of the Admiralty, Winston Churchill, across the four eastern entrances to Scapa Flow. In the immediate post-war years six of the blockships were removed and the remainder stripped to help overcome an acute steel shortage.

At the commencement of hostilities in September 1939 all coastal lights had been extinguished except for those specifically required for defence purposes. It was under these conditions that the brand-new Norwegian-registered motor vessel *Mim*, returning to Bergen with a cargo of wheat from Freemantle, grounded on the Reef Dyke, North Ronaldsay during the night of 1 November 1939. Eleven of her crew managed to reach shore in one of the ship's boats and the twenty men remaining on board were taken off by the Stromness lifeboat. It only took three days for the *Mim* to break up completely. Less than a week later, on 7 November, having been completely disabled in the North Sea by severe gales, the Bergen-registered steamer *Hansi* drifted on to the Reef Dyke, her engine-room flooded and listing heavily. She floated off on the flood tide and drove ashore in Linklet Bay. Her crew managed to abandon ship and were guided ashore by local boatmen.

Shipping losses around the Shetland Islands during the Second World War, due to enemy action and marine losses, were exactly a quarter of those experienced in the First World War. On 10 January 1940 the 3,161 ton Greek-registered steamer *Tonis Chandris*, laden with a cargo of Swedish iron ore for Barrow, ran aground on the Vere off the east coat of Unst while being chased by a German submarine. At the time of the stranding the weather was foggy and the sea calm. Over the next two days part of the cargo was jettisoned, but a tug sent from Lerwick failed to tow the ship off and she was abandoned after the weather worsened.

Severe losses were inflicted on vessels heading for and clearing Contraband Control at Kirkwall in the early months of 1940. With little in the way of anti-submarine patrols to deter them, German submarines lay off the east coast of Orkney and waited for their victims to appear. The first to be sunk was the 10,517 ton Danish motor tanker *Danmark* which was torpedoed on 12 January 1940 while at anchor in Inganess Bay just to the east of Kirkwall. A huge hole was blown in the tanker's side and the vessel sank on 22 January with her back broken. However it was still possible in July for 1,924 tons of her cargo of kerosene to be salvaged. In March the following year the forward section broke off and was refloated. After being beached in Inganess Bay for several months it was towed away for conversion to a storage hulk.

On the evening of 27 January 1940 the Norwegian steamer *Faro*, bound for Methil in ballast, was torpedoed off Orkney. The crew abandoned ship in two lifeboats and remained close to the ship, which was still afloat, before one of the boats containing eight men drifted away in the darkness. Early next morning the master decided to board his ship which was still afloat, but badly down by the head. An unsuccessful attempt was made to steer the *Faro* out to sea as, by this time, she had drifted into Taracliffe Bay, Deerness, but the propeller was far out of the water and racing. The steamer drove ashore shortly after daybreak on 28 January when the starboard anchor chain parted and the remaining crew were taken off by breeches-buoy. Later that day the missing lifeboat was washed ashore on Copinsay containing only one man alive and three bodies.

Losses continued, but the *U 53* was sunk by HMS *Gurka* on 22–23 February 1940 somewhere off Orkney. As the position given in the records plots in the middle of South Ronaldsay, it must have been an unusually high tide or the navigating officer's arithmetic was a little rusty! HMS *Gurka* was herself sunk a few months later off Norway.

On 25 May 1940, having cleared Kirkwall Contraband Control, being inward bound from Calcutta to Leith with a general cargo, the 5,667 ton Norwegian motor vessel *Tennessee* collided with the steamer *Baron Fairlie*. While trying to return to Kirkwall Bay for repairs she grounded in thick fog at Roane Bay, Deerness, on Orkney's East Mainland, on 29 May. By 4 June she had been declared a total loss so efforts were concentrated in salvaging the ship's equipment and cargo which included groundnuts and oilcake.

Because of the very severe censorship regulations in force during the war and the fragmentary nature of surviving records, very little is known about the circumstances surrounding the losses of the smaller Royal Navy casualties. For example HM Drifter *Imbat* sank off Lyness on 4 February 1941 after being involved in a collision. Neither the identity of the other ship nor whether there were any casualties is known. HM Trawler *Alberic* sank 'in the Pentland Firth' with loss of thirteen of her crew of twenty-three after colliding with the destroyer HMS *St Albans*. Although a contemporary photograph of the destroyer having her bow repaired at Lyness survives, nothing else is known about the incident. Most of the other casualties were small vessels such as anti-submarine trawlers and drifters.

One of the ships lost must have had the shortest career of the war. The *Empire Parsons* had been completed at Gray and Company's yard in West Hartlepool in October 1941. On 12 January 1942, while on her maiden voyage in ballast from the Tyne to Baltimore and leading a westbound convoy through the Pentland Firth, she ran aground at Scarton Point, Stroma, in a southeast gale with sleet showers. Fortunately none of the ships following the *Empire Parsons* went ashore. The crew were taken off by breeches-buoy and lodged in the island's school before being sent to the mainland when the weather moderated. In fact, the steamer was driven even further ashore and rapidly became a total loss. The wreck was taken over by Metal Industries and broken up. Later the same year, on 7 April the Aberdeen-registered steamer *Murrayfield* ran aground on the Peerie Bard of Mousa in dense fog on 7 April 1942 while sailing from Lerwick in ballast for Methil. With the engine-room badly holed the crew abandoned ship and, about four hours later, the steamer floated off on the flood tide and sank in deep water.

The American Liberty ship *Art Young* hard aground at Swilkie Point, Stroma 28 August 1947. (Sutherland Manson, Thurso)

As they were the subject of a major Lifeboat rescue, the circumstances surrounding the loss of HM Tug *St Olaves* and the barge *Golden Crown* at Ness of Duncansby on 21 September 1942 are well documented. The tug, with the barge in tow, grounded before daybreak in a northeast gale, torrential rain and zero visibility. Thurso lifeboat, commanded by Coxswain Neil Stewart, was called out and managed to take off twenty-four men from the barge and the crew of four from the tug in appalling conditions. Coxswain Stewart was awarded the Royal National Lifeboat Institution's Bronze Medal for this very difficult rescue.

Travellers flying into Kirkwall's Grimsetter Airport will see the rusting bows of a ship lying in the southwest corner of Inganess Bay. It belongs to the Norwegian motor tanker *Vardefjell* which broke in two in heavy weather 250 miles west of Lewis on 13 December 1941. The stern section was sighted derelict and abandoned with the engines in running order, but no means of steering. However on 28 December the forward section, with twenty-nine of the crew of forty on board, was located off the Faroes. It was not until some time in early 1942 that this section was towed into Inganess Bay and beached. The stern section was sent to the Tyne where a new bow was fitted and the last entry in the 1941 Lloyd's Loss Book for the *Vardefjell* states simply '19/7/44 Left Tyne for New York'.

In a potentially disastrous collision with an unnamed ship, the naval drifter *Rose Valley* was sunk in Weddel Sound off Flotta with a deck cargo of torpedoes on 16 December 1943. Fortunately none of the torpedoes exploded and they were all recovered, but the 100ft wooden drifter was too badly damaged to be salvaged. Today she still sits more or less upright on the bottom of Weddel Sound with a gaping hole in her stern where she was struck in the collision. The midget submarine *X-22* was lost off Dunnet Head on 7 February 1944. During exercises which were in preparation for the attack on the *Tirpitz*, the *X-22* was rammed and sunk by the submarine HMS *Syrtes*. It is not known whether there were any casualties and the precise location of the wreck is uncertain.

After the surrender of Germany in 1945 a considerable quantity of naval war material was awarded to Great Britain and this included the

765 ton displacement Geleitboot (Escort Vessel) *F2*. The design was to some extent experimental, with the high pressure boilers giving considerable problems and the ships themselves being poor seaboats. The escort vessel arrived at Scapa Flow in February 1946 and sank at her moorings in Gutter Sound on 30 December 1946. No attempt was made at the time to refloat the *F2*, but salvage work was subsequently carried out in 1968. The circumstances surrounding the loss of the ship are a complete mystery as there is no mention of her sinking in the local press or in Admiralty files lodged at the Public Record Office, Kew.

It was not until 1948 that the first post war casualty occurred when the 3,527 ton Panamanian steamer *Bellavista*, laden with a cargo of iron ore, ran aground in dense fog on 29 July at Fowl Craig, Papa Westray. Although salvage vessels were quickly on the scene, an attempt to refloat the steamer on 2 August was unsuccessful and she was abandoned two days later as a total loss. Surprisingly a few sailing vessels, usually fitted with auxiliary engines, still remained after the Second World War and carried small bulk cargoes around the seaboard of Northern Europe. The 246 ton gross Danish-registered auxiliary schooner *Nordstjernen* was on a voyage from Wismar to the Faroes with a cargo of timber when she went ashore in thick fog at the southern end of Foula on 13 November 1948. Given their extremely precarious position the crew of seven were lucky to escape in the ship's lifeboat and get ashore safely on Foula. The waters around Orkney and Shetland were obviously unlucky ones for the *Nordstjernen* as, exactly ten years previously, she had been completely disabled in a gale off Noup Head, Westray.

As in the inter-war years casualties amongst trawlers after 1945 were still extremely high, with nineteen being lost around Orkney. One of those was the *Strathelliot* of Aberdeen which grounded on the Taing of Selwick, Hoy, on 23 October 1952 while trying to shelter from a southwest gale. Her crew of twelve were only rescued with great difficulty as the Stromness Lifeboat was unable to get alongside after being struck by two huge seas and nearly capsized. The *Strathelliot* was so far off-shore that the Hoy Rocket Brigade had to have an extra line sent over from Stromness in order to reach the casualty. In the event all the crew were saved, but had to be pulled through some three hundred yards of surf.

A feature of post-war shipping in Shetland has been the large numbers of Eastern Bloc trawlers which have operated around the islands and this is reflected in the casualty figures. Thus between 1956 and 1967 a total of four Russian trawlers was lost around the islands: the *CPT 611* ashore in thick fog at Spoo Ness, Unst on 27 March 1956; the *SRT 4442 (Urbe)* wrecked Holm of Skaw, Unst on 16 October 1958 (see Chapter 9); the *Maia* aground on Broch of Houbie, Fetlar 2 February 1961, crew rescued; and the *SRT 4240* stranded on Skaw Point 4 March 1967, crew rescued.

The Pentland Firth continued to take its toll on shipping in 1960 when the 621 ton Icelandic motor vessel *Drangajökull*, homeward bound from Antwerp, capsized and sank shortly after being abandoned on 28 June. She developed a severe list after encountering heavy weather and went down about a mile and a half north of Stroma Lighthouse. An Aberdeen trawler, the *Mount Eden*, picked up the nineteen survivors who included the captain's wife and son. Shortly after midnight on 17 January 1964 the Aberdeen trawler *Rangor* ran aground on the Ness of Sound having just left Lerwick, bound for the North Sea fishing grounds. In an extremely efficient operation Lerwick Rocket Brigade had a line aboard the stranded trawler within forty minutes of her going ashore, and, an hour and a half later, all of the crew of thirteen had been rescued. Shortly after grounding the crew's quarters had caught fire, probably due to an electrical short circuit and continued to burn for the rest of the day. There was little chance of salvaging the *Rangor* and by the following Sunday only a small part of the hull was showing above water.

Even with modern navigational aids it was still possible for the 8,003 ton *Kathie Niederkirchner* to run aground on the Pentland Skerries in thick fog on 23 August 1965. The motor ship, which had only been completed the previous year, was bound for her home port of Rostock with a cargo of sugar from Havana. The crew of forty-eight and two passengers immediately abandoned ship and landed at the lighthouse where they were cared for by the keepers before being taken off by the Longhope lifeboat. Later the same day the *Kathie*

Niederkirchner slipped off the rocks on which she was lying and sank in 10 fathoms of water.

One of the great hazards of Hoy Sound are the Kirk Rocks, all too conveniently situated off Stromness Churchyard. Innumerable ships have come to grief on them with the victims being buried in the churchyard or on the 'banks' above high tide mark. The writer vividly remembers having a series of graves of drowned seamen, marked by small flagstones, lying between Warebeth and Breckness, pointed out to him by a local farmer. Fortunately, in the case of the Norwegian motor trawler *Norholmen* which grounded on the Kirk Rocks during the afternoon of 23 November 1966, the crew reached the shore safely in their liferaft and the services of the graveyard were not required. The wreck was finally driven off the Kirk Rocks during a subsequent storm and came ashore just below the graveyard where she was broken up for scrap with little now remaining except for a few twisted plates.

On 17 March 1969, while going to the aid of the stranded Liberian steamer *Irene*, the Longhope lifeboat *TGB* capsized in maelstrom conditions in the Pentland Firth and all eight men on board were lost. The 2,636 ton gross *Irene* had sailed in ballast from Granton on 13 March, bound for Glomfjord in Norway, and immediately encountered heavy weather in the North Sea. Conditions worsened even further with winds gusting to Force 11 and seas between fifty and sixty feet high being experienced by the steamer which was driven far off course towards the Scottish coast. At about nine o'clock on the evening of 17 March the *Irene*, almost out of fuel, drove ashore at Grimness on the east side of South Ronaldsay. As the steamer's position was uncertain both Kirkwall and Longhope Lifeboats were called out with mountainous confused seas and sixty foot waves being reported off Cantick Head in the Pentland Firth. Contact was lost with the Longhope lifeboat and it was found next day capsized four miles west of Torness, Hoy. Those lost on board the *TGB* included Coxswain Daniel Kirkpatrick, his two sons, and five men all from Walls in Hoy. In the meantime South Ronaldsay Rocket Brigade managed to fire a line to the *Irene* and her crew of seventeen were all safely brought ashore.

Since the Longhope lifeboat disaster, the sea has continued to take its toll of shipping around Orkney and Shetland with a total of nine trawlers and one cargo ship being lost. Three of these casualties which featured in exceptionally difficult rescues are described in Chapter Nine. In the last ten years only one vessel has been lost in the area, a far cry from the terrible decades in the middle of last century.

Salvage operations on the Norwegian steamer *Pennsylvania* stranded on Swona, 26 July 1931. One of the ship's lifeboats is launched from Swona. (Sutherland Manson, Thurso)

9

Famous Rescues

It was not until 1860 that the RNLI established its first lifeboat station in northern Scotland at Thurso. The first on Orkney was established at Stromness in 1867, followed by Longhope in 1874. Because of its remote location and the large number of shipping casualties which had occurred, the Board of Trade stationed a lifeboat at Fair Isle from 1878 till the end of the Second World War. There was an RNLI station on the Orkney island of Stronsay from 1909 to 1915 and again from 1952 to 1972.

Not until the 1930s were there any lifeboats stationed in Shetland, with the establishment of one at Lerwick in 1930 and another at Aith in 1933. This seeming delay may perhaps be seen as a tribute to the unfailing readiness of the islanders to go to the assistance of any vessels in distress.

In the early 1950s helicopters were first used in the area to rescue survivors from stranded vessels and their use since then has steadily increased. However, they have not supplanted, but rather supplemented, the search and rescue role of lifeboats. For the last century lifeboats, and latterly helicopters as well, have undertaken hundreds of services of every conceivable sort, usually in the most adverse weather conditions, and the following incidents are only a selection of the more notable rescues.

In early March 1891 the British steamer *Victoria*, on a voyage from Hamburg to New York with a general cargo, was disabled by heavy seas off the Butt of Lewis. With her pumps choked and engine room flooded, she drifted eastwards into the Pentland Firth before being spotted by a shepherd on 4 March, close inshore below the cliffs of Hoy. Longhope Lifeboat was launched and put off in a severe south-westerly gale with mountainous seas. By the time she reached the casualty, the *Victoria* was about a mile off Dunnet Head and it was impossible to get alongside to take off the crew because of the huge swell, but eventually a line was passed which enabled one of the steamer's lifeboats to safely ferry the crew of twenty-two men aboard the Longhope lifeboat. The return voyage was exceptionally difficult as the lifeboat was crammed with crew and survivors and had to battle against a full ebb tide across the most dangerous part of the Pentland Firth. It was impossible to return to base at Longhope because of the continuing gale, so the *Victoria*'s crew were landed at Herston in South Ronaldsay. The derelict steamer finally drifted ashore at Scarfskerry in Caithness and broke up immediately, with wreckage and cargo being washed up along miles of coastline. Coxswain Benjamin Stout received the RNLI's Silver Medal and a gold watch from the Emperor of Germany in recognition of the service rendered to the crew of the *Victoria* which had included eleven German seamen.

Although not carried out by lifeboat, the rescue of the survivors of the steamer *Dinnington* on the night of 16 February 1906 was also the occasion for the award of six Silver Medals by the RNLI. The 366 ton gross steamer, bound from Sunderland to Stornoway with a cargo of coal, had encountered very heavy weather in the Pentland Firth. Her master, Captain Hall, tried to put into Long Hope for shelter, but ran aground on the uninhabited island of Switha in a pitch dark night with blinding snow. The *Dinnington* started to break up almost immediately and two of her crew of eleven were washed away and drowned. The remainder launched the ship's lifeboat but it soon capsized in the surf though luckily all nine survivors managed to get ashore on Switha alive. Meanwhile the lights of the *Dinnington* had been seen by some fishermen in South Walls at the south end of Hoy. Six of them launched a yawl and sailed over to Switha to find out what had happened to the steamer. Having failed to spot the survivors in the pitch darkness they sailed over to Flotta to check there and, having drawn a blank, returned to Switha again. This time the frozen and soaked survivors were discovered huddled together in a creek from which they were rescued and landed in Flotta. For the brilliant rescue in appalling weather, all the crew of the yawl were rewarded with the RNLI's Silver Medal.

The Hull trawler *Shakespeare* was homeward bound from a successful trip to the fishing grounds off Noup Head, Westray, when she ran aground on a pitch dark morning about half a mile north of Breckness, in Stromness parish, on 11 December 1907. Alerted by the trawler's siren, the family who lived at the nearby farmhouse of Breckness raised the alarm and both the rocket brigade and lifeboat were dispatched from Stromness. By the time help arrived the hull of the *Shakespeare* was completely submerged, with survivors clinging to the tops of the masts and one unfortunate man marooned on top of the funnel. Two of the crew of ten had been swept away during an attempt to launch the trawler's lifeboat while another two had succumbed to the cold, fallen off the mizzen mast and drowned. The rocket brigade succeeded in firing a line to the three men still clinging to the mizzen mast and they were safely brought ashore. Although there was a very heavy ground swell, Stromness lifeboat managed to get in close enough to save two survivors from the foremast and then the man still perched precariously on top of the funnel. Subsequently, Coxswain Robert Greig of the Stromness lifeboat *Good Shepherd* was awarded a Silver Medal by the RNLI for this very difficult service.

Orkney's west coast was again the scene of a major rescue when the Grimsby steam trawler *Carmania II* went ashore on the Kirk Rocks, Hoy Sound early in the morning of 14 February 1929. The trawler's steering gear had been damaged while she was homeward bound from the Icelandic fishing grounds and she had gone ashore in a westerly gale with snow showers. Because of the heavy breaking seas it was not possible for the Stromness lifeboat to get alongside, so Coxswain William Johnstone started to take off the trawler's twelve-man crew by breeches-buoy. Unfortunately, after five of them had been taken off, the kedge wire (essential for keeping the breeches-buoy line taut) parted. Using the trawler's lifeboat, which had been washed overboard at the time of the stranding but was still moored alongside, the remaining seven men were ferried safely to the Stromness lifeboat. This rescue resulted in a Bronze Second Service Clasp being awarded to Coxswain Johnstone.

On 6 February 1940 the South Shields-registered steamer *High-cliffe* went ashore on Forwick Holm off Papa Stour. She was bound from Narvik with a cargo of Swedish iron ore for Immingham, her master having apparently mistaken the Neap of Norby for Fitful Head. The Aith Lifeboat was called out and stood by the stranded steamer for about four hours. Eventually twenty-eight men were taken off and landed at the master's request and the lifeboat resumed station off the casualty next day. By that time it was obvious that the steamer was a total loss so the master and six men who had remained on board abandoned ship and were landed at Aith. In all the lifeboat had been on service for over thirty hours and rescued thirty-five men.

The first major rescue of the crew of a stranded ship involving the use of helicopters was the successful operation in which forty-one men from the Norwegian ore-carrier *Dovrefjell* were airlifted to safety after the vessel had run aground on the Pentland Skerries. The 9,862 ton gross motorship had gone ashore on 3 February 1956 in a southerly gale at the east side of the Little Pentland Skerry and, because of the extremely exposed position, it was impossible for any lifeboat to get close enough to take off the crew. It was therefore decided that they should be taken off by helicopters, and a total of three were used in the operation, a Sycamore from RAF Leuchars and two Dragonflies from RNAS Fulmar, Lossiemouth. In a shuttle operation, lasting three hours, the crew of the *Dovrefjell* were taken off two or three at a time and landed at John o' Groats. Three weeks later two Metal Industries tugs succeeded in refloating the ore-carrier which, at the time of the stranding, was bound from the Tyne in ballast for Canada. After temporary repairs at Longhope the *Dovrefjell* was dry-docked at Middlesbrough where she was condemned and sold to Italian buyers.

Later the same year, on 28 December, Lerwick lifeboat took off six crewmen from the crippled Swedish motor-tanker *Samba* minutes before she was driven ashore on the Ness of Sound at Lerwick. The 663 ton gross tanker, converted from the ex-Royal Navy minesweeping trawler *Olive*, had broken down in the North Sea while on a voyage from Rotterdam to Odda in ballast. With a southerly gale blowing the Dutch tug *Noord Holland* found it impossible to take the ship in tow and, as it was approaching the east side of Shetland, managed to take off six of the crew. With the crippled tanker continuing to drift rapidly towards the shore, Lerwick Lifeboat was called out and succeeded in taking off the five men still remaining on board. Twenty minutes later, having narrowly missed grounding on Bressay in the gale force winds and very heavy seas, the *Samba* drove ashore on the Ness of Sound. Coxswain John Sales of the Lerwick Lifeboat was voted a Bronze Medal by the RNLI for this fine rescue.

Coxswain Sales was again voted an award, this time the Silver Medal, for the rescue of three Russian seamen from the Holm of Skaw, Unst, on 17 Otober 1958. The Russian trawler *Urbe* (*SRT4442*) had apparently broken down on the night of 16 October and been driven ashore in a northerly gale. Lerwick Lifeboat was called out as it was not possible for Balta Sound lifesaving apparatus to cross to the Holm because of the very heavy seas. Having taken on board a local pilot at Balta Sound, the lifeboat anchored off the casualty in the continuing gale and brought off three survivors by breeches-buoy. During the operation one of the lifeboat's propellers was fouled by a trawl net and the rescue had to be carried out on only one engine. Twenty-two men were believed to have been lost and considerable problems were experienced during the rescue because of lack of Russian co-operation. After some confusion the survivors and two bodies were handed over to Russian representatives at Balta Sound. During the service the lifeboat covered over 100 miles, with the outward leg in the teeth of a northerly gale. The local pilot, Andrew Mouat, was voted a Bronze Medal for his part in the rescue.

The mountainous west coast of Hoy was the scene of an exceptionally difficult rescue when the Longhope Lifeboat saved the crew of fourteen from the Aberdeen trawler *Strathcoe*. She had gone aground at the bottom of 400ft cliffs in a narrow cleft at the Geo of the Lame shortly after two o'clock in the morning of 4 February 1959, while returning from a nine-day fishing trip. A brief Mayday message was sent before heavy waves soaked the radio and also made the distress flares useless. By the time the lifeboat arrived huge waves were breaking over the trawler which was hard aground and listing heavily to starboard. A kedge anchor was dropped in the geo which was flanked by reefs only 150yd apart and a line fired to the casualty. The first man brought off in the breeches-buoy was washed completely out of it, but managed to hold on and was rescued by the lifeboatmen. During the early part of the rescue the trawler's small boat was washed off its chocks and narrowly missed striking the lifeboat. After waiting for the tide to fall a little, the breeches-bouy line was repositioned and the remainder of the trawler's crew successfully taken off. They were transferred to the local fishing boat *Amber Queen* and landed at Stromness. Daniel Kirkpatrick, coxswain of the Longhope Lifeboat, was voted the RNLI's Silver Medal for this very hazardous service.

Coxswain Kirkpatrick was awarded a Silver Second Service Clasp five years later when the Longhope Lifeboat rescued nine men from the stranded Aberdeen motor trawler *Ben Barvas* which had run ashore at the southern end of the Little Pentland Skerry in a pitch dark night on 3 January 1964. Five of the trawler's crew who had taken to a liferaft were picked up by the trawler *Ben Screel*. In the very heavy swell waves were breaking over the trawler which was listing heavily to port and partially submerged, with the sea around covered with floating debris and diesel oil from ruptured fuel tank. With the lifeboat anchored about 100yd from the casualty a line was fired aboard and the remaining nine men taken off by breeches-buoy. All fourteen survivors were landed at St Margaret's Hope in South Ronaldsay.

In the early hours of 19 February 1967, the Aberdeen trawler *Juniper* ran aground in Lyra Sound at the bottom of 200ft cliffs on the western side of Papa Stour. The Aith Lifeboat was called out in a southeasterly gale with rain and sleet and found the trawler ashore amongst rocks and skerries with a very heavy sea running. As it was impossible to fire a line aboard, Coxswain John Nicolson decided to run alongside the casualty and take the crew of twelve men off directly. This feat of seamanship involved steering the lifeboat through a narrow rock strewn channel, but the twelve survivors, by now cold, wet and exhausted, were safely transferred. As there was no room to turn two men were stationed as lookouts in the bows of the lifeboat and it was taken safely back out to sea through skerries and heavy breaking seas. The RNLI awarded Coxswain Nicolson its Silver Medal for this very fine rescue.

During a hurricane on 6 December 1973, the Fleetwood trawler

Navena was driven ashore on a reef some 300yd off the northern end of Copinsay on Orkney's eastern seaboard while trying to shelter from the appalling conditions. With her engine-room flooded and all main power gone, an SOS was sent out on emergency batteries. As it was impossible for any lifeboat to get near the casualty a British Airways Sikorsky S61 helicopter was scrambled from Dyce Airport, Aberdeen. When it arrived overhead the trawler was completely submerged apart from the bridge where the twelve-man crew had taken refuge. In 70 knot winds the survivors were all winched to safety in an operation lasting twenty minutes and landed at Kirkwall Airport. The crew of the helicopter and Kirkwall Coastguard, who had coordinated the rescue, were later jointly awarded the Board of Trade Rescue Shield for the best rescue involving the saving of life during 1973.

In another extremely difficult helicopter rescue, eight men were lifted to safety on 9 December 1977 when the Aberdeen trawler *Elinor Viking* stranded on the Ve Skerries. The trawler, outward bound to the northern fishing grounds, went ashore in poor visibility and storm force winds on the Clubb at the southern side of the skerries tearing a large hole in her side. With Aith Lifeboat unable to get near enough to the casualty to take off the crew, a British Airways Sikorsky helicopter was called out from Sumburgh Airport. Conditions over the stranded trawler were exceptionally bad as it was pitch dark, the cloud base was at 300ft, visibility was little over a mile and the wind was gusting from 45 to 55 knots. After searching for ten minutes the helicopter crew picked up a strong smell of diesel oil and then spotted an empty liferaft before sighting the stranded trawler. With another helicopter acting as radio link and an RAF Nimrod aircraft continually dropping flares, all of those on board the *Elinor Viking* were lifted to safety. During the rescue operation, which lasted over an hour and a half, one of the winchmen was badly bruised when he was swept against the trawler's bridge. This exceptionally difficult and dangerous rescue operation was the occasion for an unusually large number of gallantry awards being made to the crew of the rescue helicopter. Captains George Bain and Alisdair Campbell each received the Queen's Gallantry Medal with Mr Brian Johnstone and Captain Campbell Bosanquet being awarded Queen's

Commendations. In addition the crew jointly received the Coastguard Shield for 1977, the United States Aviation/Space Writers
Association and AVCO Corporation Helicopter Heroism Award and
the Prince Philip Helicopter Award of the Guild of Air Pilots and Air
Navigators.

The American cargo ship *Pioneer Commander* aground on the Pentland Skerries 13 August 1977. In the foreground are the remains of the Aberdeen trawler *Ben Barvas* wrecked 3 January 1964. (Phoenix Photos, Kirkwall)

10

Ones That Got Away

Despite the fearsome reputation of Orkney and Shetland for ship-wrecks, a surprising number of vessels have been salvaged from extraordinarily precarious positions. From the limited information available, particularly in the case of early casualties, it would appear that about ten per cent of vessels stranded around Orkney and in the Pentland Firth, were subsequently salvaged, but for the waters around Shetland and Fair Isle the figure is only about five per cent. It has to be admitted that these figures are only approximate and take no account of vessels which grounded briefly and were refloated on the next tide without suffering any damage. The chances of a stranded vessel being refloated off Shetland and Fair Isle is probably so much lower than elsewhere because they were so remote from any part of the mainland Britain, from which salvage assistance could be obtained, any casualty had usually gone to pieces by the time help had arrived. This was particularly the case in the days when ships were a great deal slower than they are today.

One of the earliest vessels salvaged was the *Sarah* of Boston, Massa-chusetts which stranded on the 'Shore of Weyland', Kirkwall on 4th May 1709. Her master petitioned the Admiralty Court for the brigan-tine's cargo to be unloaded and stored safely so that his ship might be refloated. In the case of the *Martin and Louise* of Christiansand, she had the misfortune to be stranded and 'bulged' on Bressay in Septem-ber 1753 while on a voyage from Norway to Dublin. It was found im-possible to refloat or recover the cargo (probably wood) and she was sold where she lay. However, 'when the wind turning to a particular point which occasioned a sudden swell of the sea she was raised from the rocks in a very shattered and distressed condition and she was dragged with the utmost difficulty into [Lerwick] Harbour'. In the early autumn of 1761 the *Niewe Hoop* of Amsterdam, homeward bound from Archangel, went ashore at Hamnavoe, Yell. After being discharged, she was refloated and taken to Burravoe on the same island for repair. There she was hove down (pulled over on her beam ends) for repairs to be carried out on her bottom before being reloaded and continuing on her voyage.

The brig *Taindale* of Maryport was less fortunate. She was driven ashore at Tofts Ness, Sanday by a gale on 19 November 1773. There she 'beat on the rocks for five hours' before being refloated with 5ft of water in the hold, but her cargo of logs from Riga 'was not much damaged'. However five years later in 1778 she was apparently completely wrecked on the same island while on a voyage from St Petersburg to Maryport with a cargo of flax.

On 22 December 1786 the *Geheimer Ratoon*, a Greenland whaler returning to her home port of Altona ran ashore on the Kirk Rocks, Stromness. She had on board the crews of two other whaling ships which had been lost in the pack ice and who had already undergone severe hardship, having had to subsist on blubber for several weeks after their provisions ran out. Luckily the vessel was refloated and repaired sufficiently for her to complete her voyage home.

Although not stranded, the *Karl Frederich* of Emden, with a cargo of salt from Liverpool, was abandoned off Shetland in October 1798 after losing her rudder in a storm just north of Unst. With the aid of local fishermen the vessel was brought to anchor in Burrafirth, Unst, 'in great hazard of going on the rocks'. Her master, Captain Johann Rahtske, in a letter to a local laird, Thomas Mouat of Garth, asked for assistance. 'In this my distress, I beg you will undertake to assist me in bringing the ship to a safer harbour by means of boats to tow her.'

While on a voyage from Liverpool to Gothenburg in November 1810 with a cargo of salt, the Swedish ship *Aeolus* encountered severe weather off Northern Scotland and sprang a leak. On 26 November the captain shot himself and the ship, now under the command of the mate, was beached on 29 November at Otterswick, Sanday with three feet of water in the hold, a local boat having put off and piloted her to safety. After temporary repairs it was initially decided to sail the *Aeolus* back to Liverpool for more permanent work to be carried out and four local men were signed on as temporary hands, but further survey revealed the ship to be perfectly tight and the acting-master decided to complete the original voyage to Gothenburg. The Orkneymen flatly refused to ship on board protesting that they had signed on for a voyage to Liverpool only and petitioned the Vice Admiral Depute for payment of wages due according to the original agreement. After some deliberation the men were each awarded the sum of £6 11s 6d with £2 to cover expenses.

The Prussian ship *Orion* stranded in Water Sound, Orkney on 2 December 1825 while on a voyage from Danzig with a cargo of timber for Liverpool. This particular casualty was salvaged by the brilliant Caithness engineer and salver James Bremner who, in the course of an extraordinary career, refloated and repaired no fewer than 236 vessels, one of which was the steamer *Great Britain* when she went ashore on the Irish coast. Bremner, who originally trained as a shipwright, also constructed or improved nineteen different harbours and invented various cranes, cassions and salvage equipment. In the case of the *Orion*, Bremner constructed a huge raft from her cargo of wood on to which the ship was loaded. The raft was provided with hand paddles and sails rigged on masts taken out of the ship and the whole contraption was safely sailed and rowed to Wick Bay, where the *Orion* was off-loaded and repaired. Bremner's use of this type of massive salvage pontoon anticipated by almost 150 years a similar system developed by the British firm of Risdon Beazley and was by an interesting coincidence used to transport the hulk of the *Great Britain* back from the Falkland Islands to Bristol for restoration.

In 1836 Bremner dismantled the *Lord Suffield* which had been totally wrecked on the Ness of Quoys at Canisby on the north coast of Caithness. The component pieces were then transported to his shipyard at Wick and the vessel completely rebuilt. Bremner was also involved in the salvage of the Liverpool barque *Victoria* which ran aground on the Pentland Skerries on 22 August 1849. He managed to bring ashore some of her cargo of cotton in bales before the vessel floated off unaided and after some difficulty she was taken in tow, beached at Lybster and broken up.

In the latter part of the nineteenth century, when insurance requirements were not so rigorous, local steamers often undertook the salvage of stranded or disabled vessels. Thus, when the Canadian barque *Eclipse* went ashore at Sandwick in Shetland on 9 August 1858, the local mail steamer *Prince Consort* was used to tow her off. The 964 ton barque, which was only three years old, had been on a voyage to Madras with 1,400 tons of coal when she was driven ashore in a storm with the loss of one man. After being towed to Lerwick she was bought by the trading firm of Hay and Company in 1859 before being beached and broken up at Freefield Dock. Hay & Company also bought the stranded Prussian barque *Prebislav* which had gone ashore on the island of Bigga, Yell Sound on 9 February 1870. According to the company's letter books they 'Payed fifteen men £7 10s for taking vessel off strand in Yell Sound'. The barque, which had been bound for Sunderland with a cargo of Norwegian pit-props, was taken to Lerwick where she was unloaded, stripped and used for many years as a storage hulk.

During the night of 16–17 November 1877, the Orkney Islands were struck by a terrible storm which became known locally as the *Argyllshire* gale. At least nine vessels were driven ashore and an unknown number must have foundered at sea, as huge quantities of wreckage were washed ashore. One of the largest to be stranded was the 708 ton net iron full-rigged *Argyllshire* owned by Law and Company of Glasgow which had been anchored in Hunda Sound (then known as Coburg Roads) on the east side of Scapa Flow. The ship had been on a voyage from Amsterdam to Glasgow with a cargo of hay and straw and her master, Captain Andrew Laird, a local man, having gone ashore to visit his wife and relations, was unable to return to the ship when the gale spring up. Both anchor cables parted and the *Argyllshire* drove ashore on Howquoy Head, Holm. Fortunately, no lives were lost but the ship was driven hard aground with the bottom suffering severe damage. A party of carpenters and a diver were dispatched from Glasgow and a false timber bottom was fitted. The ship suffered no further damage where she lay and was refloated the following February and beached at St Mary's, Holm. After further temporary repairs she was towed to Glasgow for a complete overhaul. Sadly, the *Argyllshire* was lost off the coast of South America a few years later.

Another casualty of the storm was the schooner *Alfred and Emma* of Lancaster. Having loaded a cargo of paving at Thurso she parted her anchor cable on 17 November and touched briefly on the rocks below Dunnet Head Lighthouse. The captain managed to swing ashore on a brace and three of the crew saved themselves in the ship's boat, leaving the unfortunate mate still aboard when the schooner drifted off into the Pentland Firth. A sail was somehow set and, about noon the same day, having run before the wind, the schooner went ashore at Dingieshowe, Deerness in the East Mainland of Orkney. Four local men put off in a boat and managed to take off the mate at considerable risk and a few days later the crew of a local fishing smack succeeded in refloating the *Alfred and Emma* and towed her to Kirkwall for repairs.

Shortly after sailing from Norway on 11 January 1884 with a cargo of 500 tons of ice for Glasgow, the Norwegian barque *Anna Christian* encountered severe weather and had to put back for repairs. Storms again dogged her when she resumed her voyage and the master finally anchored under the lee of Sound Grunay between Unst and Fetlar to take shelter. On 15 February, when the storm had moderated sufficiently, two local boatmen went aboard offering to pilot the *Anna Christian* to a safer berth. The master accepted the offer, and, after slipping both anchor cables which were fouled, the barque was safely run ashore on a soft sandy bottom at Cullivoe, Yell, taking the ground so gently that some of those on board did not realise they were no longer afloat. At the end of the month the barque was refloated undamaged.

On 20 September 1890 the iron full-rigged ship *Beecroft* of Liverpool, 1626 ton net, went ashore at Newark Bay, Sanday, in light winds and poor visibility, while on a voyage from Gavle in Sweden to Melbourne with a cargo of battens. The cargo was jettisoned and steam pumps put on board which successfully refloated the ship a week later. This was one of the largest vessels to be stranded on Sanday and the owners were extraordinarily lucky that she was salvaged from an island which was such a graveyard for shipping.

The steamer *Harlaw* (ex *Gotha*) belonging to the Aberdeen Steam Navigation Company grounded at Ness of Quoys, Caithness on 25 August 1899 while on a voyage from Aberdeen to Lerwick in ballast. Her engine-room flooded as she was holed immediately under the boilers. Fortunately the weather stayed fine and a salvage vessel was able to put steam pumps aboard three days after she had stranded. The following day 29 August, after a diver had sealed some of the leaks, she was pumped out, towed to Scrabster and beached. Damage to her machinery must have been minimal as she was able to leave for repairs in Aberdeen on 2 September under her own steam with a tug in attendance.

Given the exceptionally difficult conditions which could be encountered in the waters around Shetland, the number of serious accidents involving the local mail steamers was remarkably low, a tribute to the high standards of seamanship of those who served in them. However the mail steamer *Earl of Zetland* had the misfortune to ground on an old ballast mound while entering Balta Sound, Unst, on 10 June 1902 and stuck fast. As she settled on the falling tide a rock holed the hull in the region of the engine-room, so that she filled and sank with her maindeck awash. Fortunately she remained upright and a few days later it was possible to pump her out in about twenty minutes with equipment sent from Lerwick. With most of the damage confined to saloon and cabin furnishings it was possible for steam to be raised and, with the hole temporarily plugged, the *Earl of Zetland* was able to proceed to Lerwick under her own power for repairs and an overhaul.

During the First World War the Royal Navy mounted a total blockade of all German and Central Power ports and to maintain a complete embargo on enemy overseas trade, all vessels sailing to, or bound from, neutral ports in Northern Europe were required to pass through Contraband Control ports such as Kirkwall and Lerwick. The Copenhagen-registered steamer *Dania* was making for Kirkwall to obtain clearance for the final leg of her voyage to her home port when she grounded on Lashy Skerry off the Calf of Eday in dense fog on 13 August 1915. Work was put in hand to unload the cargo and about 100 tons of hides were landed at Stronsay after an attempt to tow the steamer off failed. On 22 August she was successfully refloated and brought into Calf Sound. By 10 September, temporary repairs having been completed, a seaworthiness certificate was granted to enable her to proceed to Copenhagen.

The Cairn Line steamer *Cairnglen* ran ashore on a reef off Huna harbour, Caithness on 23 March 1934 while passing eastbound through the Inner Sound between Stroma and St John's Point. She had been bound for the Tyne with a general cargo including a consignment of flour from Halifax, Nova Scotia. As she had gone ashore at high water it was necessary to lighten her and part of her cargo was transferred into small steamers moored alongside. Fortunately the weather stayed calm and she was towed off a few days later by the tug *Seaman* before being taken to Lyness. There it was discovered that her boilers and turbines had been displaced so she had to be towed to the Tyne for major repairs. Less than a month later, early in the morning of 13 April, the German motor tanker *Kattegat* stranded on Tor Ness, Hoy in a southeast gale and driving rain with a cargo of crude oil and gasoline from Texas for Stockholm. Fortunately she was able to refloat herself and proceed to Lyness under her own power for examination by divers. The local newspapers reported that the tanker was dressed overall on 20 April, Hitler's birthday, with the crew marching to Lyness Naval Cemetery to lay a wreath on the graves of German seamen buried there. After transferring her cargo to another tanker and sealing her tanks the *Kattegat* then sailed on 24 April for Germany as she was too badly damaged for local repairs to be carried out.

It was not until August 1947 that the first post-war casualties occurred when two ships went ashore in the Pentland Firth in dense fog. The first was the Norwegian tanker *Gundine* (ex *Cyprus Hill Park*) which grounded on Hoy between Green Head and Berry Head with a cargo of heavy crude oil on 23 August. In an attempt to refloat his ship the captain simply pumped 1,500 tons of his cargo over the side and she was able to get off under her own power about eight hours after stranding. The effect on the local bird life was catastrophic, with most of the western coast of Hoy suffering severe pollution. Stromness lifeboat, which had stood by the casualty, had to be cleaned with paraffin and hosed down by the local fire brigade when she returned to base. Although extensively damaged the *Gundine* was able to continue on her voyage to Copenhagen. Less than a week later, on 28 August, the Liberty ship *Art Young* of Pensacola, while passing through the Pentland Firth westbound, went ashore on the Swilkie Point, Stroma. She was firmly ashore but three large tugs managed to tow her off next day.

The Swedish motor tanker *Oljaren*, 8,337 tons gross, ran aground on the Muckle Pentland Skerry on 12 April 1951 in an exceptionally dangerous and exposed position, having been caught by the very strong currents and swept off course. The tanker, bound from Curaçao with a cargo of diesel oil for Stockholm, was holed in the bow and started to leak. The crew of forty were taken off in a severe gale by the Longhope Lifeboat in a service lasting over thirty-six hours for which the Coxswain Alfred Johnstone was awarded a Bronze Medal by the RNLI. In order to refloat the tanker salvage staff from Metal Industries pumped compressed air into sealed sections of her hull and she was successfully towed off on 30 April by the tug *Salveda*.

In 1977 the Pentland Skerries were again the scene of a successful salvage operation when the American cargo ship *Pioneer Commander* was refloated from the Louther Skerry. The ship, owned by the United States Lines, had sailed from Bremerhaven on 11 August with a cargo of military stores for Bayonne, New Jersey. Shortly before two o'clock on the morning of 13 August she ran aground at 16 knots on a sloping shelf of rock in patchy fog and steadily decreasing visibility. As the weather remained calm the crew stayed aboard and, during the following week, she was deballasted, with some of her oil bunkers being transferred to a small tanker. At high water on the morning of 20 August she was refloated with the assistance of the Dutch tug *Typhoon* and taken to Lyness for survey. It was found that the entire bottom had been effectively ripped open and the ship was floating on her tank tops. She was drydocked at Wallsend-on-Tyne where a completely new bottom was built.

Two years later, at 1am on 29 July 1979, the Liberian-registered bulk carrier *Vida*, fully laden with 30,000 tons of iron ore, broke down in the Pentland Firth close to Swona. As it was impossible to repair the damage and, with the ship drifting rapidly towards the dreaded Tarf Tail, the crew abandoned ship. They were picked up by the BP tanker *Springer* and landed at Scrabster. In the meantime the

Vida had drifted eastwards with the tide narrowly missing Swona. About two hours after the *Vida* had been abandoned the Orkney Towage Company tug *Kessock* managed to get a line aboard and tow her to Sinclair Bay undamaged. Thereafter she was taken to Kirkwall Bay and a fractured fuel pipe, the cause of the breakdown, repaired so that she could continue on her voyage.

Salvage operation on the Cairn Line steamer *Cairnglen* which went ashore at Huna, Caithness on 23 March 1934.

APPENDIX A
Trade Patterns

From an analysis of voyage details from 240 wrecks it is possible to classify origins, cargoes and destinations into seven general categories.

Origins	Cargoes	Destinations
Eastland—Russia plus empire and Sweden	Wood and iron	UK and Europe
North Europe— Holland, Hanse Ports and Denmark	Cloth, manufactured goods, linseed, flax and grain	East and West Indies, UK and South Europe
UK (export and coastwise)	Coal, salt, cotton goods, slates and pavement	Russia, Scandinavia, North Europe and UK
North America— America and Canada	Sugar, cotton, tobacco, oil products and timber	Scandinavia, Russia North Europe and UK
Scandinavia	Timber, iron and steel	UK, North America and Australia
Whale Fisheries— Greenland and Davis Straits	Whale oil and whale products	Holland, Hanse Ports and UK
The Indies	Fabrics, spices, luxury goods and tea	Holland and Scandinavia

These trade patterns confirm those described
by the late Tom Henderson in an analysis of
Shetland shipwrecks. Precise figures are not
available, but by volume it would appear that
timber from Russia, the Baltic states and
Scandinavia was by far the largest item of
cargo carried until well into the nineteenth
century. Of the British exports, salt shipped
from Liverpool and coal were the most
important cargoes. The north European trade
of the seventeenth and eighteenth centuries
was aimed at two separate markets: fabrics
and manufactured goods were exported to
colonies and trading posts in the Indies where
they were exchanged for exotic woods, fine
fabrics, spices and luxury goods such as
porcelain; in the other branch, linseed, flax
and grain were shipped to Great Britain and
southern Europe.

THE SEVENTEENTH AND EIGHTEENTH CENTURY
TRADE ROUTES AROUND NORTH SCOTLAND

1	NORTH AMERICAN	whale fisheries, wood
2	NORTH RUSSIAN	wood, tar, flax, hemp, iron
3	AMERICAS	tobacco, sugar, cotton
4	LIVERPOOL	salt, cotton goods
5	COASTWISE	coal, grain
6	NORTH EUROPE	cloth, grain, linseed, flax, manufactured goods
7	EAST LAND	(sweden and russian empire) wood, iron
8	EAST INDIES	fabrics, spices, luxurury goods

faroe

shetland

orkney

Seventeenth and eighteenth century trade routes around
Northern Scotland, reconstructed from voyage details of 240
shipwrecks in Orkney

APPENDIX B

Shipping Losses by Decade

The seemingly low levels of casualties before 1760 may be more apparent than real in the case of Orkney, with information almost entirely lacking on shipwrecks in the Pentland Firth. Thereafter they take off rapidly in both areas, reflecting the great increase in shipping activity which coincided with the start of the British industrial revolution. During the Napoleonic Wars a considerable volume of shipping was diverted north-about Britain to avoid problems with French privateers operating in the English Channel. The severe economic slump at the end of hostilities and the re-establishment of normal trading routes are reflected in the massive decrease in casualties from 1811–40. The eventual huge upturn in trade is marked by the unsurpassed peak in losses for the decade 1841–50 caused in part by the still very incomplete coverage of coastal lights. With improved coverage, and steam replacing sail, casualty rates declined steadily thereafter in the following decades. In the latter part of the nineteenth century changing trade patterns also tended to route ships away from the Shetland Islands, as has happened to Orkney in the latter part of the twentieth century.

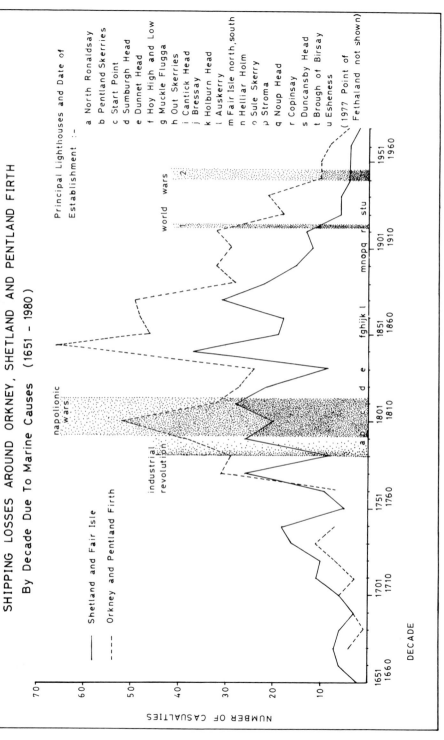

Shipping losses due to marine causes by decade for Orkney and Shetland 1651–1980

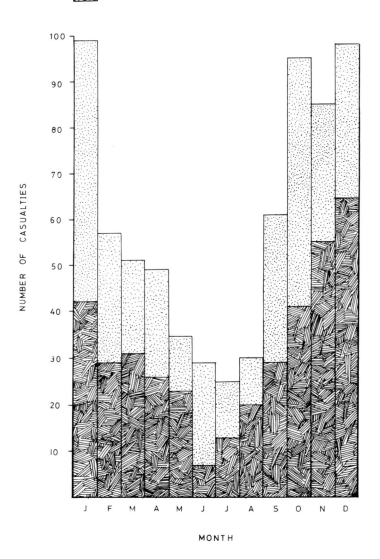

Monthly losses due to marine causes for Orkney and Shetland

APPENDIX C

Losses by Month

As would be expected losses show a strong
correlation with the time of year, low levels
being experienced during the months of
maximum daylight, while over eighty per cent
of the casualties occurred in the seven months
from September to March. Put simply, the
seaman's enemies in spring and summer were
fogs for steamships and calms for sailing
vessels, while in autumn and winter all the
hazards of darkness, gales, blizzards and poor
visibility were combined to produce
conditions which were positively lethal until
the advent of electronic navigational aids.

APPENDIX D

The *Crown* Proclamation

Forsameikle[1] as there (have been) Many of the passengers and
seamen that hath escaped of the vessel late broken at Deirsound and
called the *Crown* come into this town and some of them have (been)
quhered[2] to prejudge and wrong the Inhabitants. In remead qrof[3]
these are in his Majesties name and authoritie and in name and
authoritie of the Provost and bailyies[4] of the said burgh, Discharging
the haill Inhabitants within the same to arrest of any of the said crew
except such civel persones as the receavers of them will be ansyerable
for and give notice of thr names nightlie to any of the Magistrats in
qais[5] quarter they live, or to the Clerk that notice may be had of thr
names and qualifications. Certifieing thes quha[6] dueth in the Contrair
they shall be lyable for any prejudice the saids strayling persones shall
doe by, and auth[r] such censure as shall be thought couverment for
their contempt and disobedience qrof none is to pnd[7] ignorance Be
these(?) puts.[8] Given under the hand of our Clerk of the said burgh
the 17 day of De[r] 1679.

God save the King

(Signed) Da. Forbes Cl.[9]

17 Der 1679 this proclamed by W[m] Angussone officer and W[m]
Marwick drummer for qch[10] given at the provest direction 12s out of
Jaes adamesones wyfes fyne.

1. forasmuch	6. who
2. heard	7. pretend
3. whereof	8. presents (i.e. this proclamation, a legal term)
4. aldermen	9. Clerk
5. whose	10. which

Proclamation referring to *Crown* 'broken at Deirsound', Orkney on 10 December 1679 when over two hundred Covenanters lost their lives. A transcription is given opposite (Orkney Library Archive)

APPENDIX E

Protected Shetland Islands Wreck Sites

At the instigation of the late Tom Henderson, then Curator of the Shetland Museum, the Zetland County Council, predecessor to the Shetland Island Council, leased from the Commissioners of Crown Lands the seabed rights of fourteen areas where important wrecks were known to be located. It has therefore been possible for the local council to exert strict control over the wrecks and prevent them from being looted by treasure hunters. The following is a list of the fourteen protected wrecks, preceded by their date of loss, taken from Tom Henderson's paper on shipwrecks and underwater archaeology in Shetland.

1567   *Unicorn* Scottish frigate, off Tingwall
1588   *El Gran Grifon* Armada hulk, Fair Isle
1588?   Unknown vessel possibly from Armada, off Reawick
1653   *Lastdrager* Dutch East Indiaman, Yell
1664   *Kennemerland* Dutch East Indiaman, Out Skerries
1687   *Wrangles Palais* Danish warship, Out Skerries
1701   *Duiker* Dutch armed whaler, Uyea, North-mavine
1711   *Liefde* Dutch East Indiaman, Out Skerries
1729   *Curacao* Dutch warship, off Unst
1737   *Vendela* Danish East Indiaman, Fetlar
1744   *Abraham* Dutch armed ship, Uyea, North-mavine
1745   *Stockholm* Swedish East Indiaman, Dunrossness
1780   *Evstafii* Russian warship, Whalsay
1786   *Concordia* Danish East Indiaman, Cunningsburgh

The Death of a Ship

The remarkable sequence of photographs on
the following pages was taken by Mr Tom
Rosie, a former resident of Swona. It shows
the end of the Swedish motor ship *Gunnaren*
which went ashore on Swona in thick fog on
19 August 1935. (Photographs Stromness
Museum)

The tug in the photograph attempts to tow the *Gunnaren* off...

But during the salvage attempts the ship breaks its back...

Pounding seas then break the ship in two...

...and the stern section is swept ashore.

Bibliography

Unpublished Sources

Prior to the nineteenth century, responsibility for shipwrecks around the coasts of Scotland was vested in the Crown, who, for reasons of penury or gratitude, parcelled out the various offices of Admiral and Vice Admiral to private individuals. Records of early shipwrecks thus tend to be dispersed through an immense variety of sources such as estate papers, legal processes, private correspondence and commercial records. It was not until 1847 that central government started to systematically collect information and issue statistics on shipping casualties. The following unpublished sources have been consulted:

Shetland

Bruce of Symbister Papers
Irvine of Midbrake Papers
The Papers of E. S. Reid Tait
Customs and Excise Records (Lerwick Outport)
Sheriff Court Records (Lerwick)
Gardie Papers
Hay and Company (Lerwick) Limited, Records

Orkney

Balfour Papers
Watt of Breckness Papers
Taylor Papers
Earldom of Orkney Papers

Papers of Messrs Macrae and Robertson
Traill Dennison Papers
Customs and Excise Records (Kirkwall Outport)
Morton Papers
Sutherland-Graeme Papers
Stanley Cursiter Papers
Justice of the Peace Records (Kirkwall)
Sheriff Court Records (Kirkwall)
Admiralty Court Records (Kirkwall)

Edinburgh

Scarth of Breckness Muniments
Mey Papers
Inventory of Orkney and Shetland Papers
Records of Privy Council

London

Admiralty Files, Public Record Office, Kew

Books

The published sources listed below are the principal ones consulted and will give the reader who wishes to pursue the subject further a broad background.

Adams, I. H. and Fortune, C. *Alexander Lindsay, A Rutter of the Scottish Seas c1540* (National Maritime Museum No44, 1980)
Allardyce, Keith and Hood, Evelyn M. *At Scotland's Edge* (Collins, 1986)
Bruce, R. Stuart. 'Some old-time Shetlandic Wrecks', *Old Lore Miscellany of Orkney, Shetland, Caithness and Sutherland* (Viking Society, various issues 1907–1912)
Colledge, J. J. *Ships of the Royal Navy* (David and Charles, 1970, two volumes)
Collins, Captain Greenville. *Great Britain's Coasting Pilot* (London, 1693)

Dennison, Julie. *The Dutch Ship* (unpublished manuscript, 1985)

Dittmar, E. J. and Colledge, J. J. *British Warships 1914–19* (Ian Allan, 1972)

Donaldson, Gordon. *Shetland Life Under Earl Patrick* (Oliver and Boyd, 1958)

Eunson, Jerry. *The Shipwrecks of Fair Isle* (W. S. Wilson, undated)

Fea, James. *The Present State of the Orkney Islands* (Edinburgh, 1775)

Ferguson, David M. *The Wrecks of Scapa Flow* (Orkney Press, 1985)

Goodfellow, Alexander. *Sanday Church History* (W. R. Mackintosh, 1912)

Gossett, W. P. *The Lost Ships of the Royal Navy 1793–1900* (Mansell Publishing, 1986)

Grant, Robert M. *U-Boat Intelligence 1914–1918* (Putnam, 1969)

Gröner, Erich. *Die deutschen Kriegschiffe 1815–1945* (J. F. Leman's Verlag, 1966)

Henderson, Tom. 'Shipwreck and Underwater Archaeology in Shetland', *Shetland Archaeology* Brian Smith, editor (Shetland Times, 1985)

Hewison, W. S. *This Great Harbour Scapa Flow* (Orkney Press, 1985)

Hocking, Charles (editor). *Dictionary of Disasters at Sea during the age of Steam 1824–1962* (Lloyds Register of Shipping, 1969, two volumes)

Mackenzie, Murdo. *Orcades: or a Geographic and Hydrographic Survey of the Orkney and Lewis Islands* (London, 1750)

Martin, Colin. *Full Fathom Five* (Chatto and Windus, 1975)

Martin, Simon. *The Other Titanic* (David and Charles, 1980)

Morrison, Ian. *The North Sea Earls* (Gentry Books, 1973)

Mowat, John. *James Bremner Wreck Raiser* (John Humphreys, undated)

Muckelroy, Keith (editor). *Archaeology under Water* (McGraw-Hill, 1980)

Nicolson, James R. *Shetland* (David and Charles, 1972)

Pottinger, J. *For Those in Peril* (Stromness Museum, 1975)

Price, Richard and Muckelroy, Keith. 'The second season of work on the Kennemerland site 1973', *The International Journal of Nautical Archaeology and Underwater Exploration* (1974 3.w:257–268)

Robson, Adam. *Saga of a Ship, Earl of Zetland* (The Shetland Times, 1982)

Sinclair, Sir John (editor). *The Statistical Account of Scotland 1791–1799* Vol XIX Orkney and Shetland (EP Publishing, 1978)

Tulloch, Peter A. *A Window on North Ronaldsay* (The Kirkwall Press, 1974)

van der Vat, D. *The Grand Scuttle* (Hodder and Stoughton, 1982)

von Munching, L. L. *Merchant Shipping Losses of Allied, Neutral and Central Powers, during and shortly after World War One* (Department of Defence (The Hague), 1968)

Wilson, Bryce. *The Lighthouses of Orkney* (Stromness Museum, 1975)

British Vessels Lost at Sea 1914–18 (Patrick Stephens, 1972)

British Vessels Lost at Sea 1939–45 (Patrick Stephens, 1983)
Merchant Shipping 1913–14: Return of Shipping Casualties and Loss of Life for the Year Ended 30 June 1914. Cmd 984 (HMSO, 1920)
Merchant Shipping 1 July 1914–31 December 1918: Return of Shipping Casualties and Loss of Life for the Period Ended 31 December 1918. Cmd 1089 (HMSO, 1921)
North Coast of Scotland Pilot (Hydrographic Department, Ministry of Defence, 1975)
The Diary of the Reverend John Mill, Shetland 1740–1803 (University Press Edinburgh, 1889)
'Wreck of the Kennemerland', *Exploration and Discovery by the Aston University Sub Aqua Club* (University of Aston in Birmingham, 1974)

Periodicals

Aberdeen Chronicle
Aberdeen Free Press
Aberdeen Herald
Aberdeen Weekly Journal
Caithness Courier
Edinburgh Evening Courant
John o'Groat Journal
Lloyds List
Lloyds Register of Shipping
Lloyds Weekly Casualty Reports
Manson's Shetland Almanac
Northern Ensign
Orcadian
Orkney and Shetland Journal
Orkney Herald
Press and Journal
Proceedings of Orkney Antiquarian Society
Scotsman
Shetland News
Shetland Times
The Lifeboat

Acknowledgements

Covering as it does a very large area, it would have been impossible to have written this book without the assistance and encouragement of many people. In particular I would like to thank the following: James Wilson, Stromness, for allowing me to record his memories of the scuttling of the German Fleet; Miss P. van Anrooj of the Algemeen Rijksarchief, The Hague, for locating material on the Dutch frigate *Utrecht*; P. C. Jalhay, Afdeling Maritieme Historie, The Hague, Allison Fraser of Orkney Library Archives for her immense assistance in locating relevant records; Brian Smith of Shetland Archives for providing a huge amount of material and advice on further sources; Andrew Williamson, Curator of Shetland Museum, for information on Shetland shipwrecks and correcting my more deplorable errors; Sutherland Manson, Thurso, for his reminiscences of a Stroma boyhood and details of Pentland Firth shipwrecks; Robert Leask, Lerwick, for providing information on 'The Shuggar Ship' and other wrecks at Bigton, Dunrossness; Eddie Gunn, Wick, for access and use of the *John o' Groat Journal* card index; Bryce Wilson, Museums Officer, Orkney Islands Council, for permission to use material from Stromness Museum; Isabella Deans, Local Studies Department, Aberdeen Central Library, for information on early local periodicals; Chris Henderson, Lerwick, for data on Shetland shipwrecks; James Nicolson, Scalloway, for information and advice on a huge variety of queries; Philip Thomas of Thornliebank, for information on sources of nineteenth century wreck statistics, and Orkney Library for permission to use material from the Ernest Marwick Tape Collection, Orkney Sound Archive.

Assistance from the following institutes and persons is also gratefully acknowledged: The Mitchell Library, Glasgow; The Orkney

148

Library, Kirkwall; The Shetland Library, Lerwick; Woodside Library, Aberdeen; Wick Library, Caithness; Thurso Library, Caithness; Register House, Edinburgh; Information Section, Lloyd's Register of Shipping, London; Sandy Tait, Stromness; Sandy Young, Stromness; Mrs Kathy Wilson, Stromness; Dr Raymond Lamb, Kirkwall; Tom McCallum, Stromness; John Broom, Stromness; John Edwards, Aberdeen; Kevin Henry, Aith; Magnus Shearer, Honorary Secretary, Lerwick Lifeboat; Lieutenant Commander T. Moniz, US Coastguard, Washington DC; J. William Spence, Kirkwall; James MacLean, Surveyor, HM Customs and Excise, Kirkwall; John Bruce, Registrar, HM Customs and Excise, Kirkwall; James Ferguson, Aberdeen; D. Linklater, RNLI Headquarters, Poole; John Ballantyne, Edinburgh; Andy Carter, Lerwick and Mrs A Dinger-Telle, Portlethen.

The wreck of the German immigrant ship *Lessing*, which went ashore on 23 May 1868, dwarfed by the towering cliffs at Clavers Geo, Fair Isle. (Shetland Museum)

Index of Ships Wrecked

(**Note** (s) indicates vessel salvaged)

Dione	1906	Schooner, Swedish	55–6
Dolphin	1727	Brig, British	35–6
Dovre	1913	Steamer, Norwegian	68
Dovrefjell(s)	1956	Ore carrier, Norw.	115
Drangajökull	1960	Motor vessel, Icelandic	108
Dresden	1919	Cruiser, German	86
Duke of Sussex	1840	Ship, British	46
Duna	1912	Steamer, British	67–8
Duncan	1877	Steamer, British	61–2
Dunrobin	1862	Unknown, British	50
E49, HMS	1917	Submarine, British	75
Eagle	1862	Schooner, British	50
Earl of Zetland(s)	1902	Mail steamer, British	126
Eclipse(s)	1858	Barque, Canadian	124
Edenmore	1909	Ship, British	56, 59
Edina	1830	Schooner, British	45
Elfin	1862	Brigantine, British	50
Elgen	1897	Steamer, Norwegian	64–5
Elinor Viking	1977	Motor trawler, Brit.	118–9
Ellida	1864	Schooner, Norwegian	51
Empire Parsons	1942	Steamer, British	104
Empire Seaman (ex *Morea*)	1940	Steamer, British	102
F2	1946	Geleitboote, Ger.	106–7
Faro	1940	Steamer, Norwegian	103
Fidelia	1864	Schooner, Prussian	52
Fifa	1148	Longship, Viking	29
Flyderborg	1917	Steamer, Danish	76
Fortuna	1848	Barque, Russian	48
Fredrich der Grosse(s)	1919	Battleship, German	82
Freia	1864	Barque, Norwegian	51
G89(s)	1919	Destroyer, German	84
Geheimer Ratoon(s)	1786	Whaler, Danish	122
Gezina	1863	Galliot, German	50–1

General Index

159